The Essential

Air Fryer

Cookbook for Beginners 2024

1900 Days of Easy, Delicious, and Budget-Friendly Recipes Book | Quick 15-Minute Cooking Guide for Frying, Baking, Grilling, and More

Pascalle Megens

• Table of Content

● Introduction

Unleash Your Culinary Creativity with the Air Fryer Cookbook

Welcome to a new era of cooking with the Air Fryer Cookbook, where indulgent flavors meet healthy living. Imagine biting into perfectly crispy fries, tender chicken wings, or golden-brown pastries—all made with a fraction of the oil used in traditional frying methods. This cookbook is your passport to a world where you can enjoy your favorite dishes guilt-free and with ease.

A Culinary Revolution at Your Fingertips

The Air Fryer Cookbook is not just another recipe collection; it's your gateway to a culinary revolution. With the power of air frying, you can transform everyday ingredients into extraordinary meals. This cookbook is designed to take you on a flavorful journey, where each recipe is crafted to bring out the best in your food, making healthy eating both enjoyable and exciting.

The Magic of Air Frying

Air frying is more than a healthier alternative; it's a game-changer for your kitchen. By using rapid air technology, the air fryer circulates hot air around your food to achieve that perfect crispiness without the need for excessive oil. This means you can enjoy all the deliciousness of fried foods with significantly fewer calories and fats. It's a win-win for your taste buds and your health.

Why You'll Love the Air Fryer Cookbook

At the heart of this cookbook is the air fryer, a versatile appliance that opens up endless culinary possibilities. With features like adjustable cooking times and temperatures, as well as dual cooking zones, you can prepare multiple dishes at once without mixing flavors. This makes meal preparation not only healthier but also more efficient and fun.

What You'll Learn

Cooking Techniques: Master the art of air frying with our detailed guides. Learn the optimal temperatures and cooking times for different foods, ensuring perfect results every time.

Flavor Boosters: Discover how to enhance your dishes with marinades, spices, and coatings that bring out the best in your ingredients.

Maintenance Tips: Keep your air fryer in top condition with our easy-to-follow maintenance and cleaning tips, ensuring it remains a staple in your kitchen for years to come.

A Culinary Journey from Start to Finish

Our cookbook is packed with a wide variety of recipes that cater to every craving:

Appetizers: Delight in crispy appetizers like garlic parmesan wings and spicy cauliflower bites that are perfect for starting any meal.

Main Courses: Indulge in mouthwatering mains such as juicy steak, tender salmon, and savory stuffed peppers that will satisfy your hunger and taste amazing.

Sides and Snacks: Enjoy perfectly cooked sides like truffle fries and roasted vegetables, or snack on crispy chickpeas and homemade kale chips.

Desserts: Satisfy your sweet tooth with air-fried treats like cinnamon sugar donuts and molten chocolate cakes that are both delicious and healthier.

Transform Your Kitchen Experience

Ready to revolutionize your cooking and enjoy delicious, healthier meals? The Air Fryer Cookbook is your ultimate guide to mastering this innovative appliance. Embrace the convenience and versatility of air frying, and discover how it can transform your everyday meals into culinary masterpieces. Let's make every meal an adventure in flavor and health together!

What is Air Frying?

An air fryer represents a revolutionary appliance

in modern kitchens, functioning as a compact convection oven that fits neatly on your countertop. Unlike traditional frying methods that submerge food in oil, an air fryer utilizes rapid hot air circulation to achieve a crispy exterior while retaining moisture inside. This innovative cooking process significantly reduces the need for oil, promoting healthier meals without sacrificing taste or texture.

The Evolution and Appeal of Air Fryers

While the concept of cooking with hot air dates back decades, the first commercial air fryer emerged in the 2010s, marking a milestone in culinary technology. Initially simplistic, today's air fryers have evolved with advanced features and expanded cooking capacities, catering to diverse culinary needs. They now come in various designs, equipped with accessories such as grill pans and baking trays, enhancing their versatility and functionality in the kitchen.

Why Air Fryers Have Become Popular

Air fryers have garnered widespread popularity worldwide due to several compelling advantages:

Health Consciousness: By using little to no oil, air fryers provide a healthier cooking option, appealing to individuals seeking to reduce calorie intake and fat consumption.

Versatility: From crispy chicken wings to roasted vegetables and even desserts, air fryers handle a wide array of recipes, offering convenience and flexibility for diverse culinary experiments.

Time Efficiency: With rapid heating and intuitive controls, air fryers streamline meal preparation, enabling quick and hassle-free cooking while preserving food's natural flavors.

Crispy Results: Air frying achieves a satisfyingly crispy texture similar to deep-frying, but with minimal oil, allowing for guilt-free indulgence in favorite crispy dishes.

Easy Maintenance: Most air fryers feature removable, dishwasher-safe parts and non-stick surfaces, ensuring effortless cleanup and reducing kitchen cleanup time.

Odor Control: By using hot air instead of oil, air fryers produce less smoke and cooking odors, creating a more pleasant cooking environment suitable for any space.

Space Efficiency: Compact in size, air fryers occupy minimal countertop space, making them ideal for apartments, smaller kitchens, or anyone seeking to optimize kitchen space.

Tips for Getting Started with Your Air Fryer:

Preheat with Purpose: Just like an oven, preheating your air fryer is essential for achieving optimal results. This step ensures even cooking and helps to achieve that coveted crispy texture.

Mind the Space: Avoid overcrowding the air fryer basket or tray. Leaving enough room between food items allows for proper air circulation, which is crucial for even cooking and ensuring your dishes come out crispy all around.

Shake and Shuffle: About halfway through the cooking time, shake the basket or gently shuffle the food around on the tray. This simple step helps to ensure that all sides of the food are exposed to the hot air, promoting even browning and crispiness.

A Light Touch of Oil: While air frying requires significantly less oil than traditional frying, a light coating can enhance flavor and texture. Consider using an oil mister or brush to apply a thin layer of oil to your food before cooking.

Temperature and Timing: Each air fryer model can behave differently. Experiment with different temperature settings and cooking times to find what works best for you and your favorite recipes. Start with the recommended settings in your air fryer's manual and adjust as needed based on your preferences and the type of food you are preparing.

Clean and Maintain: Proper maintenance ensures your air fryer remains in top condition. After each use, clean the basket or tray with warm, soapy water or in the dishwasher if it's dishwasher-safe. Wipe down the interior and exterior of the air fryer with a damp cloth, and follow the manufacturer's instructions for deeper cleaning and maintenance.

With these practical tips, you'll quickly become adept at using your air fryer to create delicious, crispy meals with ease. Enjoy exploring the versatility of air frying and discovering new ways to prepare healthier versions of your favorite dishes.

Here are some tips for maintaining your air fryer:

Regular Cleaning Routine: After each use, clean the basket and tray thoroughly with a damp cloth or sponge. This removes any leftover food particles and grease, preventing them from affecting future cooking sessions. Ensure they are completely dry before storing to avoid mold or rust.

Monthly Deep Cleaning: Schedule a deep clean at least once a month, or as recommended by the manufacturer. Disassemble removable parts and clean them meticulously to maintain hygiene and optimal performance. Follow the specific cleaning instructions provided in the user manual to avoid damaging the appliance.

Choosing Gentle Cleaning Products: Opt for mild dish soap when cleaning your air fryer.

Avoid harsh chemicals or abrasive cleaners that could scratch the non-stick coating or exterior finish. Use a soft cloth or sponge to preserve the appliance's surfaces.

Keeping Electrical Components Dry: Never immerse the main unit in water or expose it to excessive moisture. Use a damp cloth to wipe down the exterior, ensuring the control panel and electrical parts remain dry and undamaged.

Proper Storage Practices: Store your air fryer in a cool, dry place when not in use. Avoid stacking heavy items on top of it and keep it away from direct heat sources to prevent physical damage and maintain its appearance.

Timely Replacement of Parts: Regularly inspect your air fryer for signs of wear, such as cracked baskets or worn-out trays. Replace any damaged parts promptly to ensure optimal cooking performance and safety.

By following these maintenance tips, you'll prolong the lifespan of your air fryer and continue to enjoy delicious, crispy meals with ease.

● CHAPTER 1 Breakfast Delights

Bacon and Cheese Quiche

Preparation time: 5 minutes | Cook time: 12 minutes | Serves 2

- 3 large eggs
- 2 tablespoons heavy whipping cream
- ¼ teaspoon salt
- 4 slices cooked sugar-free bacon, crumbled
- ½ cup shredded mild Cheddar cheese

Instructions

1. In a large bowl, whisk eggs, cream, and salt together until combined. Mix in bacon and Cheddar. 2. Pour mixture evenly into two ungreased ramekins. Place into air fryer basket. Adjust the temperature to 320°F (160°C) and bake for 12 minutes. Quiche will be fluffy and set in the middle when done. 3. Let quiche cool in ramekins 5 minutes. Serve warm.

Johnny Cakes

Preparation time: 10 minutes | Cook time: 10 to 12 minutes | Serves 4

- ½ cup all-purpose flour
- 1½ cups yellow cornmeal
- 2 tablespoons sugar
- 1 teaspoon baking powder
- 1 teaspoon salt
- 1 cup milk, whole or 2%
- 1 tablespoon butter, melted
- 1 large egg, lightly beaten
- 1 to 2 tablespoons oil

Instructions

1. In a large bowl, whisk the flour, cornmeal, sugar, baking powder, and salt until blended. Whisk in the milk, melted butter, and egg until the mixture is sticky but still lumpy. 2. Preheat the air fryer to 350°F (177°C). Line the air fryer basket with parchment paper. 3. For each cake, drop 1 heaping tablespoon of batter onto the parchment paper. The fryer should hold 4 cakes. 4. Spritz the cakes with oil and cook for 3 minutes. Turn the cakes, spritz with oil again, and cook for 2 to 3 minutes more. Repeat with a second batch of cakes.

Strawberry Tarts

Preparation time: 15 minutes | Cook time: 10 minutes | Serves 6

- 2 refrigerated piecrusts
- ½ cup strawberry preserves
- 1 teaspoon cornstarch
- Cooking oil spray
- ½ cup low-fat vanilla yogurt
- 1 ounce (28 g) cream cheese, at room temperature
- 3 tablespoons confectioners' sugar
- Rainbow sprinkles, for decorating

Instructions

1. Place the piecrusts on a flat surface. Using a knife or pizza cutter, cut each piecrust into 3 rectangles, for 6 total. Discard any unused dough from the piecrust edges. 2. In a small bowl, stir together the preserves and cornstarch. Mix well, ensuring there are no lumps of cornstarch remaining. 3. Scoop 1 tablespoon of the strawberry mixture onto the top half of each piece of piecrust. 4. Fold the bottom of each piece up to enclose the filling. Using the back of a fork, press along the edges of each tart to seal. 5. Insert the crisper plate into the basket and the basket into the unit. Preheat the unit by selecting BAKE, setting the temperature to 375°F (191°C), and setting the time to 3 minutes. Select START/STOP to begin. 6. Once the unit is preheated, spray the crisper plate with cooking oil. Working in batches, spray the breakfast tarts with cooking oil and place them into the basket in a single layer. Do not stack the tarts. 7. Select BAKE, set the temperature to 375°F (191°C), and set the time to 10 minutes. Select START/STOP

to begin. 8. When the cooking is complete, the tarts should be light golden brown. Let the breakfast tarts cool fully before removing them from the basket. 9. Repeat steps 5, 6, 7, and 8 for the remaining breakfast tarts. 10. In a small bowl, stir together the yogurt, cream cheese, and confectioners' sugar. Spread the breakfast tarts with the frosting and top with sprinkles.

Turkey Sausage Breakfast Pizza

Preparation time: 15 minutes | Cook time: 24 minutes | Serves 2

- ➤ 4 large eggs, divided
- ➤ 1 tablespoon water
- ➤ ½ teaspoon garlic powder
- ➤ ½ teaspoon onion powder
- ➤ ½ teaspoon dried oregano
- ➤ 2 tablespoons coconut flour
- ➤ 3 tablespoons grated Parmesan cheese
- ➤ ½ cup shredded provolone cheese
- ➤ 1 link cooked turkey sausage, chopped (about 2 ounces / 57 g)
- ➤ 2 sun-dried tomatoes, finely chopped
- ➤ 2 scallions, thinly sliced

Instructions

1. Preheat the air fryer to 400°F (204°C). Line a cake pan with parchment paper and lightly coat the paper with olive oil. 2. In a large bowl, whisk 2 of the eggs with the water, garlic powder, onion powder, and dried oregano. Add the coconut flour, breaking up any lumps with your hands as you add it to the bowl. Stir the coconut flour into the egg mixture, mixing until smooth. Stir in the Parmesan cheese. Allow the mixture to rest for a few minutes until thick and dough-like. 3. Transfer the mixture to the prepared pan. Use a spatula to spread it evenly and slightly up the sides of the pan. Air fry until the crust is set but still light in color, about 10 minutes. Top with the cheeses, sausage, and sun-dried tomatoes. 4. Break the remaining 2 eggs into a small bowl, then slide them onto the pizza. Return the pizza to the air fryer. Air fry 10 to 14 minutes until the egg whites are set and the yolks are the desired doneness. Top with the scallions and allow to rest for 5 minutes before serving.

Butternut Squash and Ricotta Frittata

Preparation time: 10 minutes | Cook time: 33 minutes | Serves 2 to 3

- ➤ 1 cup cubed (½-inch) butternut squash (5½ ounces / 156 g)
- ➤ 2 tablespoons olive oil
- ➤ Kosher salt and freshly ground black pepper, to taste
- ➤ 4 fresh sage leaves, thinly sliced
- ➤ 6 large eggs, lightly beaten
- ➤ ½ cup ricotta cheese
- ➤ Cayenne pepper

Instructions

1. In a bowl, toss the squash with the olive oil and season with salt and black pepper until evenly coated. Sprinkle the sage on the bottom of a cake pan and place the squash on top. Place the pan in the air fryer and bake at 400°F (204°C) for 10 minutes. Stir to incorporate the sage, then cook until the squash is tender and lightly caramelized at the edges, about 3 minutes more. 2. Pour the eggs over the squash, dollop the ricotta all over, and sprinkle with cayenne. Bake at 300°F (149°C) until the eggs are set and the frittata is golden brown on top, about 20 minutes. Remove the pan from the air fryer and cut the frittata into wedges to serve.

Turkey Breakfast Sausage Patties

Preparation time: 5 minutes | Cook time: 10 minutes | Serves 4

- ➤ 1 tablespoon chopped fresh thyme
- ➤ 1 tablespoon chopped fresh sage
- ➤ 1¼ teaspoons kosher salt
- ➤ 1 teaspoon chopped fennel seeds
- ➤ ¾ teaspoon smoked paprika
- ➤ ½ teaspoon onion powder
- ➤ ½ teaspoon garlic powder
- ➤ ⅛ teaspoon crushed red pepper flakes
- ➤ ⅛ teaspoon freshly ground black pepper
- ➤ 1 pound (454 g) 93% lean ground turkey
- ➤ ½ cup finely minced sweet apple

(peeled)

Instructions

1. Thoroughly combine the thyme, sage, salt, fennel seeds, paprika, onion powder, garlic powder, red pepper flakes, and black pepper in a medium bowl. 2. Add the ground turkey and apple and stir until well incorporated. Divide the mixture into 8 equal portions and shape into patties with your hands, each about ¼ inch thick and 3 inches in diameter. 3. Preheat the air fryer to 400°F (204°C). 4. Place the patties in the air fryer basket in a single layer. You may need to work in batches to avoid overcrowding. 5. Air fry for 5 minutes. Flip the patties and air fry for 5 minutes, or until the patties are nicely browned and cooked through. 6. Remove from the basket to a plate and repeat with the remaining patties. 7. Serve warm.

Buffalo Chicken Breakfast Muffins

Preparation time: 7 minutes | Cook time: 13 to 16 minutes | Serves 10

➤ 6 ounces (170 g) shredded cooked chicken
➤ 3 ounces (85 g) blue cheese, crumbled
➤ 2 tablespoons unsalted butter, melted
➤ ⅓ cup Buffalo hot sauce, such as Frank's RedHot
➤ 1 teaspoon minced garlic
➤ 6 large eggs
➤ Sea salt and freshly ground black pepper, to taste
➤ Avocado oil spray

Instructions

1. In a large bowl, stir together the chicken, blue cheese, melted butter, hot sauce, and garlic. 2. In a medium bowl or large liquid measuring cup, beat the eggs. Season with salt and pepper. 3. Spray 10 silicone muffin cups with oil. Divide the chicken mixture among the cups, and pour the egg mixture over top. 4. Place the cups in the air fryer and set to 300°F (149°C). Bake for 13 to 16 minutes, until the muffins are set and cooked through. (Depending on the size of your air fryer, you may need to cook the muffins in batches.)

Tomato and Cheddar Rolls

Preparation time: 30 minutes | Cook time: 25 minutes | Makes 12 rolls

➤ 4 Roma tomatoes
➤ ½ clove garlic, minced
➤ 1 tablespoon olive oil
➤ ¼ teaspoon dried thyme
➤ Salt and freshly ground black pepper, to taste
➤ 4 cups all-purpose flour
➤ 1 teaspoon active dry yeast
➤ 2 teaspoons sugar
➤ 2 teaspoons salt
➤ 1 tablespoon olive oil
➤ 1 cup grated Cheddar cheese, plus more for sprinkling at the end
➤ 1½ cups water

Instructions

1. Cut the Roma tomatoes in half, remove the seeds with your fingers and transfer to a bowl. Add the garlic, olive oil, dried thyme, salt and freshly ground black pepper and toss well. 2. Preheat the air fryer to 390°F (199°C). 3. Place the tomatoes, cut side up in the air fryer basket and air fry for 10 minutes. The tomatoes should just start to brown. Shake the basket to redistribute the tomatoes, and air fry for another 5 to 10 minutes at 330°F (166°C) until the tomatoes are no longer juicy. Let the tomatoes cool and then rough chop them. 4. Combine the flour, yeast, sugar and salt in the bowl of a stand mixer. Add the olive oil, chopped roasted tomatoes and Cheddar cheese to the flour mixture and start to mix using the dough hook attachment. As you're mixing, add 1¼ cups of the water, mixing until the dough comes together. Continue to knead the dough with the dough hook for another 10 minutes, adding enough water to the dough to get it to the right consistency. 5. Transfer the dough to an oiled bowl, cover with a clean kitchen towel and let it rest and rise until it has doubled in volume, about 1 to 2 hours. Then, divide the dough into 12 equal portions. Roll each portion of dough into a ball. Lightly coat each

dough ball with oil and let the dough balls rest and rise a second time, covered lightly with plastic wrap for 45 minutes. (Alternately, you can place the rolls in the refrigerator overnight and take them out 2 hours before you bake them.) 6. Preheat the air fryer to 360°F (182°C). 7. Spray the dough balls and the air fryer basket with a little olive oil. Place three rolls at a time in the basket and bake for 10 minutes. Add a little grated Cheddar cheese on top of the rolls for the last 2 minutes of air frying for an attractive finish.

Sausage Egg Cup

Preparation time: 10 minutes | Cook time: 15 minutes | Serves 6

➢ 12 ounces (340 g) ground pork breakfast sausage
➢ 6 large eggs
➢ ½ teaspoon salt
➢ ¼ teaspoon ground black pepper
➢ ½ teaspoon crushed red pepper flakes

Instructions

1. Place sausage in six 4-inch ramekins (about 2 ounces / 57 g per ramekin) greased with cooking oil. Press sausage down to cover bottom and about ½-inch up the sides of ramekins. Crack one egg into each ramekin and sprinkle evenly with salt, black pepper, and red pepper flakes. 2. Place ramekins into air fryer basket. Adjust the temperature to 350°F (177°C) and set the timer for 15 minutes. Egg cups will be done when sausage is fully cooked to at least 145°F (63°C) and the egg is firm. Serve warm.

Pumpkin Donut Holes

Preparation time: 15 minutes | Cook time: 14 minutes | Makes 12 donut holes

➢ 1 cup whole-wheat pastry flour, plus more as needed
➢ 3 tablespoons packed brown sugar
➢ ½ teaspoon ground cinnamon
➢ 1 teaspoon low-sodium baking powder
➢ ⅓ cup canned no-salt-added pumpkin purée (not pumpkin pie filling)
➢ 3 tablespoons 2% milk, plus more as needed
➢ 2 tablespoons unsalted butter, melted
➢ 1 egg white
➢ Powdered sugar (optional)

Instructions

1. In a medium bowl, mix the pastry flour, brown sugar, cinnamon, and baking powder. 2. In a small bowl, beat the pumpkin, milk, butter, and egg white until combined. Add the pumpkin mixture to the dry ingredients and mix until combined. You may need to add more flour or milk to form a soft dough. 3. Divide the dough into 12 pieces. With floured hands, form each piece into a ball. 4. Cut a piece of parchment paper or aluminum foil to fit inside the air fryer basket but about 1 inch smaller in diameter. Poke holes in the paper or foil and place it in the basket. 5. Put 6 donut holes into the basket, leaving some space around each. Air fry at 360°F (182°C) for 5 to 7 minutes, or until the donut holes reach an internal temperature of 200°F (93°C) and are firm and light golden brown. 6. Let cool for 5 minutes. Remove from the basket and roll in powdered sugar, if desired. Repeat with the remaining donut holes and serve.

Pancake for Two

Preparation time: 5 minutes | Cook time: 30 minutes | Serves 2

➢ 1 cup blanched finely ground almond flour
➢ 2 tablespoons granular erythritol
➢ 1 tablespoon salted butter, melted
➢ 1 large egg
➢ ⅓ cup unsweetened almond milk
➢ ½ teaspoon vanilla extract

Instructions

1. In a large bowl, mix all ingredients together, then pour half the batter into an ungreased round nonstick baking dish. 2. Place dish into air fryer basket. Adjust the temperature to 320°F (160°C) and bake for 15 minutes. The pancake will be golden brown on top and firm, and a toothpick inserted in the center will come out clean when done. Repeat with remaining batter. 3. Slice in half in dish and

serve warm.

Pita and Pepperoni Pizza

Preparation time: 10 minutes | Cook time: 6 minutes | Serves 1

- 1 teaspoon olive oil
- 1 tablespoon pizza sauce
- 1 pita bread
- 6 pepperoni slices
- ¼ cup grated Mozzarella cheese
- ¼ teaspoon garlic powder
- ¼ teaspoon dried oregano

Instructions

1. Preheat the air fryer to 350°F (177°C). Grease the air fryer basket with olive oil. 2. Spread the pizza sauce on top of the pita bread. Put the pepperoni slices over the sauce, followed by the Mozzarella cheese. 3. Season with garlic powder and oregano. 4. Put the pita pizza inside the air fryer and place a trivet on top. 5. Bake in the preheated air fryer for 6 minutes and serve.

Spaghetti Squash Fritters

Preparation time: 15 minutes | Cook time: 8 minutes | Serves 4

- 2 cups cooked spaghetti squash
- 2 tablespoons unsalted butter, softened
- 1 large egg
- ¼ cup blanched finely ground almond flour
- 2 stalks green onion, sliced
- ½ teaspoon garlic powder
- 1 teaspoon dried parsley

Instructions

1. Remove excess moisture from the squash using a cheesecloth or kitchen towel. 2. Mix all ingredients in a large bowl. Form into four patties. 3. Cut a piece of parchment to fit your air fryer basket. Place each patty on the parchment and place into the air fryer basket. 4. Adjust the temperature to 400°F (204°C) and set the timer for 8 minutes. 5. Flip the patties halfway through the cooking time. Serve warm.

Meritage Eggs

Preparation time: 5 minutes | Cook time: 8 minutes | Serves 2

- 2 teaspoons unsalted butter (or coconut oil for dairy-free), for greasing the ramekins
- 4 large eggs
- 2 teaspoons chopped fresh thyme
- ½ teaspoon fine sea salt
- ¼ teaspoon ground black pepper
- 2 tablespoons heavy cream (or unsweetened, unflavored almond milk for dairy-free)
- 3 tablespoons finely grated Parmesan cheese (or Kite Hill brand chive cream cheese style spread, softened, for dairy-free)
- Fresh thyme leaves, for garnish (optional)

Instructions

1. Preheat the air fryer to 400°F (204°C). Grease two (4 ounces / 113 g) ramekins with the butter. 2. Crack 2 eggs into each ramekin and divide the thyme, salt, and pepper between the ramekins. Pour 1 tablespoon of the heavy cream into each ramekin. Sprinkle each ramekin with 1½ tablespoons of the Parmesan cheese. 3. Place the ramekins in the air fryer and bake for 8 minutes for soft-cooked yolks (longer if you desire a harder yolk). 4. Garnish with a sprinkle of ground black pepper and thyme leaves, if desired. Best served fresh.

Egg and Bacon Muffins

Preparation time: 5 minutes | Cook time: 15 minutes | Serves 1

- 2 eggs
- Salt and ground black pepper, to taste
- 1 tablespoon green pesto
- 3 ounces (85 g) shredded Cheddar cheese
- 5 ounces (142 g) cooked bacon
- 1 scallion, chopped

Instructions

1. Preheat the air fryer to 350°F (177°C). Line a cupcake tin with parchment paper. 2. Beat the eggs with pepper, salt, and pesto in a bowl. Mix in the

cheese. 3. Pour the eggs into the cupcake tin and top with the bacon and scallion. 4. Bake in the preheated air fryer for 15 minutes, or until the egg is set. 5. Serve immediately.

Red Pepper and Feta Frittata

Preparation time: 10 minutes | Cook time: 20 minutes | Serves 4

- ➤ Olive oil cooking spray
- ➤ 8 large eggs
- ➤ 1 medium red bell pepper, diced
- ➤ ½ teaspoon salt
- ➤ ½ teaspoon black pepper
- ➤ 1 garlic clove, minced
- ➤ ½ cup feta, divided

Instructions

1. Preheat the air fryer to 360°F(182°C). Lightly coat the inside of a 6-inch round cake pan with olive oil cooking spray. 2. In a large bowl, beat the eggs for 1 to 2 minutes, or until well combined. 3. Add the bell pepper, salt, black pepper, and garlic to the eggs, and mix together until the bell pepper is distributed throughout. 4. Fold in ¼ cup of the feta cheese. 5. Pour the egg mixture into the prepared cake pan, and sprinkle the remaining ¼ cup of feta over the top. 6. Place into the air fryer and bake for 18 to 20 minutes, or until the eggs are set in the center. 7. Remove from the air fryer and allow to cool for 5 minutes before serving.

Parmesan Ranch Risotto

Preparation time: 10 minutes | Cook time: 30 minutes | Serves 2

- ➤ 1 tablespoon olive oil
- ➤ 1 clove garlic, minced
- ➤ 1 tablespoon unsalted butter
- ➤ 1 onion, diced
- ➤ ¾ cup Arborio rice
- ➤ 2 cups chicken stock, boiling
- ➤ ½ cup Parmesan cheese, grated

Instructions

1. Preheat the air fryer to 390°F (199°C). 2. Grease a round baking tin with olive oil and stir in the garlic, butter, and onion. 3. Transfer the tin to the air fryer and bake for 4 minutes. Add the rice and bake for 4 more minutes. 4. Turn the air fryer to 320°F (160°C) and pour in the chicken stock. Cover and bake for 22 minutes. 5. Scatter with cheese and serve.

Peppered Maple Bacon Knots

Preparation time: 5 minutes | Cook time: 7 to 8 minutes | Serves 6

- ➤ 1 pound (454 g) maple smoked center-cut bacon
- ➤ ¼ cup maple syrup
- ➤ ¼ cup brown sugar
- ➤ Coarsely cracked black peppercorns, to taste

Instructions

1. Preheat the air fryer to 390°F (199°C). 2. On a clean work surface, tie each bacon strip in a loose knot. 3. Stir together the maple syrup and brown sugar in a bowl. Generously brush this mixture over the bacon knots. 4. Working in batches, arrange the bacon knots in the air fryer basket. Sprinkle with the coarsely cracked black peppercorns. 5. Air fry for 5 minutes. Flip the bacon knots and continue cooking for 2 to 3 minutes more, or until the bacon is crisp. 6. Remove from the basket to a paper towel-lined plate. Repeat with the remaining bacon knots. 7. Let the bacon knots cool for a few minutes and serve warm.

Simple Cinnamon Toasts

Preparation time: 5 minutes | Cook time: 4 minutes | Serves 4

- ➤ 1 tablespoon salted butter
- ➤ 2 teaspoons ground cinnamon
- ➤ 4 tablespoons sugar
- ➤ ½ teaspoon vanilla extract
- ➤ 10 bread slices

Instructions

1. Preheat the air fryer to 380°F (193°C). 2. In a bowl, combine the butter, cinnamon, sugar, and vanilla extract. Spread onto the slices of bread. 3. Put the bread inside the air fryer and bake for 4 minutes or until golden brown. 4. Serve warm.

Egg Muffins

Preparation time: 10 minutes | Cook time: 11 to 13 minutes | Serves 4

- ➢ 4 eggs
- ➢ Salt and pepper, to taste
- ➢ Olive oil
- ➢ 4 English muffins, split
- ➢ 1 cup shredded Colby Jack cheese
- ➢ 4 slices ham or Canadian bacon

Instructions

1. Preheat the air fryer to 390°F (199°C). 2. Beat together eggs and add salt and pepper to taste. Spray a baking pan lightly with oil and add eggs. Bake for 2 minutes, stir, and continue cooking for 3 or 4 minutes, stirring every minute, until eggs are scrambled to your preference. Remove pan from air fryer. 3. Place bottom halves of English muffins in air fryer basket. Take half of the shredded cheese and divide it among the muffins. Top each with a slice of ham and one-quarter of the eggs. Sprinkle remaining cheese on top of the eggs. Use a fork to press the cheese into the egg a little so it doesn't slip off before it melts. 4. Air fry at 360°F (182°C) for 1 minute. Add English muffin tops and cook for 2 to 4 minutes to heat through and toast the muffins.

Mozzarella Bacon Calzones

Preparation time: 15 minutes | Cook time: 12 minutes | Serves 4

- ➢ 2 large eggs
- ➢ 1 cup blanched finely ground almond flour
- ➢ 2 cups shredded Mozzarella cheese
- ➢ 2 ounces (57 g) cream cheese, softened and broken into small pieces
- ➢ 4 slices cooked sugar-free bacon, crumbled

Instructions

1. Beat eggs in a small bowl. Pour into a medium nonstick skillet over medium heat and scramble. Set aside. 2. In a large microwave-safe bowl, mix flour and Mozzarella. Add cream cheese to the bowl. 3. Place bowl in microwave and cook 45 seconds on high to melt cheese, then stir with a fork until a soft dough ball forms. 4. Cut a piece of parchment to fit air fryer basket. Separate dough into two sections and press each out into an 8-inch round. 5. On half

of each dough round, place half of the scrambled eggs and crumbled bacon. Fold the other side of the dough over and press to seal the edges. 6. Place calzones on ungreased parchment and into air fryer basket. Adjust the temperature to 350°F (177°C) and set the timer for 12 minutes, turning calzones halfway through cooking. Crust will be golden and firm when done. 7. Let calzones cool on a cooking rack 5 minutes before serving.

All-in-One Toast

Preparation time: 10 minutes | Cook time: 10 minutes | Serves 1

- ➢ 1 strip bacon, diced
- ➢ 1 slice 1-inch thick bread
- ➢ 1 egg
- ➢ Salt and freshly ground black pepper, to taste
- ➢ ¼ cup grated Colby cheese

Instructions

1. Preheat the air fryer to 400°F (204°C). 2. Air fry the bacon for 3 minutes, shaking the basket once or twice while it cooks. Remove the bacon to a paper towel lined plate and set aside. 3. Use a sharp paring knife to score a large circle in the middle of the slice of bread, cutting halfway through, but not all the way through to the cutting board. Press down on the circle in the center of the bread slice to create an indentation. 4. Transfer the slice of bread, hole side up, to the air fryer basket. Crack the egg into the center of the bread, and season with salt and pepper. 5. Adjust the air fryer temperature to 380°F (193°C) and air fry for 5 minutes. Sprinkle the grated cheese around the edges of the bread, leaving the center of the yolk uncovered, and top with the cooked bacon. Press the cheese and bacon into the bread lightly to help anchor it to the bread and prevent it from blowing around in the air fryer. 6. Air fry for one or two more minutes, just to melt the cheese and finish cooking the egg. Serve immediately.

Sausage Stuffed Poblanos

Preparation time: 15 minutes | Cook time: 15 minutes | Serves 4

- ➢ ½ pound (227 g) spicy ground pork

breakfast sausage

- ➤ 4 large eggs
- ➤ 4 ounces (113 g) full-fat cream cheese, softened
- ➤ ¼ cup canned diced tomatoes and green chiles, drained
- ➤ 4 large poblano peppers
- ➤ 8 tablespoons shredded Pepper Jack cheese
- ➤ ½ cup full-fat sour cream

Instructions

1. In a medium skillet over medium heat, crumble and brown the ground sausage until no pink remains. Remove sausage and drain the fat from the pan. Crack eggs into the pan, scramble, and cook until no longer runny. 2. Place cooked sausage in a large bowl and fold in cream cheese. Mix in diced tomatoes and chiles. Gently fold in eggs. 3. Cut a 4-inch to 5-inch slit in the top of each poblano, removing the seeds and white membrane with a small knife. Separate the filling into four servings and spoon carefully into each pepper. Top each with 2 tablespoons pepper jack cheese. 4. Place each pepper into the air fryer basket. 5. Adjust the temperature to 350°F (177°C) and set the timer for 15 minutes. 6. Peppers will be soft and cheese will be browned when ready. Serve immediately with sour cream on top.

Breakfast Pita

Preparation time: 5 minutes | Cook time: 6 minutes | Serves 2

- ➤ 1 whole wheat pita
- ➤ 2 teaspoons olive oil
- ➤ ½ shallot, diced
- ➤ ¼ teaspoon garlic, minced
- ➤ 1 large egg
- ➤ ¼ teaspoon dried oregano
- ➤ ¼ teaspoon dried thyme
- ➤ ⅛ teaspoon salt
- ➤ 2 tablespoons shredded Parmesan cheese

Instructions

1. Preheat the air fryer to 380°F(193°C). 2. Brush the top of the pita with olive oil, then spread the diced shallot and minced garlic over the pita. 3. Crack the egg into a small bowl or ramekin, and season it with oregano, thyme, and salt. 4. Place the pita into the air fryer basket, and gently pour the egg onto the top of the pita. Sprinkle with cheese over the top. 5. Bake for 6 minutes. 6. Allow to cool for 5 minutes before cutting into pieces for serving.

Baked Potato Breakfast Boats

Preparation time: 10 minutes | Cook time: 20 minutes | Serves 4

- ➤ 2 large russet potatoes, scrubbed
- ➤ Olive oil
- ➤ Salt and freshly ground black pepper, to taste
- ➤ 4 eggs
- ➤ 2 tablespoons chopped, cooked bacon
- ➤ 1 cup shredded Cheddar cheese

Instructions

1. Poke holes in the potatoes with a fork and microwave on full power for 5 minutes. 2. Turn potatoes over and cook an additional 3 to 5 minutes, or until the potatoes are fork-tender. 3. Cut the potatoes in half lengthwise and use a spoon to scoop out the inside of the potato. Be careful to leave a layer of potato so that it makes a sturdy "boat." 4. Preheat the air fryer to 350°F (177°C). 5. Lightly spray the air fryer basket with olive oil. Spray the skin side of the potatoes with oil and sprinkle with salt and pepper to taste. 6. Place the potato skins in the air fryer basket, skin-side down. Crack one egg into each potato skin. 7. Sprinkle ½ tablespoon of bacon pieces and ¼ cup of shredded cheese on top of each egg. Sprinkle with salt and pepper to taste. 8. Air fry until the yolk is slightly runny, 5 to 6 minutes, or until the yolk is fully cooked, 7 to 10 minutes.

Breakfast Meatballs

Preparation time: 10 minutes | Cook time: 15 minutes | Makes 18 meatballs

- ➤ 1 pound (454 g) ground pork breakfast sausage
- ➤ ½ teaspoon salt
- ➤ ¼ teaspoon ground black pepper
- ➤ ½ cup shredded sharp Cheddar cheese

- ➢ 1 ounce (28 g) cream cheese, softened
- ➢ 1 large egg, whisked

Instructions

1. Combine all ingredients in a large bowl. Form mixture into eighteen 1-inch meatballs. 2. Place meatballs into ungreased air fryer basket. Adjust the temperature to 400°F (204°C) and air fry for 15 minutes, shaking basket three times during cooking. Meatballs will be browned on the outside and have an internal temperature of at least 145°F (63°C) when completely cooked. Serve warm.

Gyro Breakfast Patties with Tzatziki

Preparation time: 10 minutes | Cook time: 20 minutes per batch | Makes 16 patties

- ➢ Patties:
- ➢ 2 pounds (907 g) ground lamb or beef
- ➢ ½ cup diced red onions
- ➢ ¼ cup sliced black olives
- ➢ 2 tablespoons tomato sauce
- ➢ 1 teaspoon dried oregano leaves
- ➢ 1 teaspoon Greek seasoning
- ➢ 2 cloves garlic, minced
- ➢ 1 teaspoon fine sea salt
- ➢ Tzatziki:
- ➢ 1 cup full-fat sour cream
- ➢ 1 small cucumber, chopped
- ➢ ½ teaspoon fine sea salt
- ➢ ½ teaspoon garlic powder, or 1 clove garlic, minced
- ➢ ¼ teaspoon dried dill weed, or 1 teaspoon finely chopped fresh dill
- ➢ For Garnish/Serving:
- ➢ ½ cup crumbled feta cheese (about 2 ounces / 57 g)
- ➢ Diced red onions
- ➢ Sliced black olives
- ➢ Sliced cucumbers

Instructions

1. Preheat the air fryer to 350°F (177°C). 2. Place the ground lamb, onions, olives, tomato sauce, oregano, Greek seasoning, garlic, and salt in a large bowl. Mix well to combine the ingredients. 3. Using your hands, form the mixture into sixteen 3-inch patties. Place about 5 of the patties in the air fryer and air fry for 20 minutes, flipping halfway through. Remove the patties and place them on a serving platter. Repeat with the remaining patties. 4. While the patties cook, make the tzatziki: Place all the ingredients in a small bowl and stir well. Cover and store in the fridge until ready to serve. Garnish with ground black pepper before serving. 5. Serve the patties with a dollop of tzatziki, a sprinkle of crumbled feta cheese, diced red onions, sliced black olives, and sliced cucumbers. 6. Store leftovers in an airtight container in the refrigerator for up to 5 days or in the freezer for up to a month. Reheat the patties in a preheated 390°F (199°C) air fryer for a few minutes, until warmed through.

Pancake Cake

Preparation time: 10 minutes | Cook time: 7 minutes | Serves 4

- ➢ ½ cup blanched finely ground almond flour
- ➢ ¼ cup powdered erythritol
- ➢ ½ teaspoon baking powder
- ➢ 2 tablespoons unsalted butter, softened
- ➢ 1 large egg
- ➢ ½ teaspoon unflavored gelatin
- ➢ ½ teaspoon vanilla extract
- ➢ ½ teaspoon ground cinnamon

Instructions

1. In a large bowl, mix almond flour, erythritol, and baking powder. Add butter, egg, gelatin, vanilla, and cinnamon. Pour into a round baking pan. 2. Place pan into the air fryer basket. 3. Adjust the temperature to 300°F (149°C) and set the timer for 7 minutes. 4. When the cake is completely cooked, a toothpick will come out clean. Cut cake into four and serve.

Cheddar Soufflés

Preparation time: 15 minutes | Cook time: 12 minutes | Serves 4

- ➢ 3 large eggs, whites and yolks separated
- ➢ ¼ teaspoon cream of tartar

- ➤ ½ cup shredded sharp Cheddar cheese
- ➤ 3 ounces (85 g) cream cheese, softened

Instructions

1. In a large bowl, beat egg whites together with cream of tartar until soft peaks form, about 2 minutes. 2. In a separate medium bowl, beat egg yolks, Cheddar, and cream cheese together until frothy, about 1 minute. Add egg yolk mixture to whites, gently folding until combined. 3. Pour mixture evenly into four ramekins greased with cooking spray. Place ramekins into air fryer basket. Adjust the temperature to 350°F (177°C) and bake for 12 minutes. Eggs will be browned on the top and firm in the center when done. Serve warm.

Asparagus and Bell Pepper Strata

Preparation time: 10 minutes | Cook time: 14 to 20 minutes | Serves 4

- ➤ 8 large asparagus spears, trimmed and cut into 2-inch pieces
- ➤ ⅓ cup shredded carrot
- ➤ ½ cup chopped red bell pepper
- ➤ 2 slices low-sodium whole-wheat bread, cut into ½-inch cubes
- ➤ 3 egg whites
- ➤ 1 egg
- ➤ 3 tablespoons 1% milk
- ➤ ½ teaspoon dried thyme

Instructions

1. In a baking pan, combine the asparagus, carrot, red bell pepper, and 1 tablespoon of water. Bake in the air fryer at 330°F (166°C) for 3 to 5 minutes, or until crisp-tender. Drain well. 2. Add the bread cubes to the vegetables and gently toss. 3. In a medium bowl, whisk the egg whites, egg, milk, and thyme until frothy. 4. Pour the egg mixture into the pan. Bake for 11 to 15 minutes, or until the strata is slightly puffy and set and the top starts to brown. Serve.

Fried Cheese Grits

Preparation time: 10 minutes | Cook time: 10 to 12 minutes | Serves 4

- ➤ ⅔ cup instant grits
- ➤ 1 teaspoon salt

- ➤ 1 teaspoon freshly ground black pepper
- ➤ ¾ cup whole or 2% milk
- ➤ 3 ounces (85 g) cream cheese, at room temperature
- ➤ 1 large egg, beaten
- ➤ 1 tablespoon butter, melted
- ➤ 1 cup shredded mild Cheddar cheese
- ➤ Cooking spray

Instructions

1. Mix the grits, salt, and black pepper in a large bowl. Add the milk, cream cheese, beaten egg, and melted butter and whisk to combine. Fold in the Cheddar cheese and stir well. 2. Preheat the air fryer to 400°F (204°C). Spray a baking pan with cooking spray. 3. Spread the grits mixture into the baking pan and place in the air fryer basket. 4. Air fry for 10 to 12 minutes, or until the grits are cooked and a knife inserted in the center comes out clean. Stir the mixture once halfway through the cooking time. 5. Rest for 5 minutes and serve warm.

Bourbon Vanilla French Toast

Preparation time: 15 minutes | Cook time: 6 minutes | Serves 4

- ➤ 2 large eggs
- ➤ 2 tablespoons water
- ➤ ⅔ cup whole or 2% milk
- ➤ 1 tablespoon butter, melted
- ➤ 2 tablespoons bourbon
- ➤ 1 teaspoon vanilla extract
- ➤ 8 (1-inch-thick) French bread slices
- ➤ Cooking spray

Instructions

1. Preheat the air fryer to 320°F (160°C). Line the air fryer basket with parchment paper and spray it with cooking spray. 2. Beat the eggs with the water in a shallow bowl until combined. Add the milk, melted butter, bourbon, and vanilla and stir to mix well. 3. Dredge 4 slices of bread in the batter, turning to coat both sides evenly. Transfer the bread slices onto the parchment paper. 4. Bake for 6 minutes until nicely browned. Flip the slices halfway through the cooking time. 5. Remove from the basket to a plate and repeat with the remaining 4 slices of bread. 6. Serve

warm.

Quesadillas

Preparation time: 10 minutes | Cook time: 15 minutes | Serves 4

- ➤ 4 eggs
- ➤ 2 tablespoons skim milk
- ➤ Salt and pepper, to taste
- ➤ Oil for misting or cooking spray
- ➤ 4 flour tortillas
- ➤ 4 tablespoons salsa
- ➤ 2 ounces (57 g) Cheddar cheese, grated
- ➤ ½ small avocado, peeled and thinly sliced

Instructions

1. Preheat the air fryer to 270°F (132°C). 2. Beat together eggs, milk, salt, and pepper. 3. Spray a baking pan lightly with cooking spray and add egg mixture. 4. Bake for 8 to 9 minutes, stirring every 1 to 2 minutes, until eggs are scrambled to your liking. Remove and set aside. 5. Spray one side of each tortilla with oil or cooking spray. Flip over. 6. Divide eggs, salsa, cheese, and avocado among the tortillas, covering only half of each tortilla. 7. Fold each tortilla in half and press down lightly. 8. Place 2 tortillas in air fryer basket and air fry at 390°F (199°C) for 3 minutes or until cheese melts and outside feels slightly crispy. Repeat with remaining two tortillas. 9. Cut each cooked tortilla into halves or thirds.

Pumpkin Spice Muffins

Preparation time: 10 minutes | Cook time: 15 minutes | Serves 6

- ➤ 1 cup blanched finely ground almond flour
- ➤ ½ cup granular erythritol
- ➤ ½ teaspoon baking powder
- ➤ ¼ cup unsalted butter, softened
- ➤ ¼ cup pure pumpkin purée
- ➤ ½ teaspoon ground cinnamon
- ➤ ¼ teaspoon ground nutmeg
- ➤ 1 teaspoon vanilla extract
- ➤ 2 large eggs

Instructions

1. In a large bowl, mix almond flour, erythritol, baking powder, butter, pumpkin purée, cinnamon, nutmeg, and vanilla. 2. Gently stir in eggs. 3. Evenly pour the batter into six silicone muffin cups. Place muffin cups into the air fryer basket, working in batches if necessary. 4. Adjust the temperature to 300°F (149°C) and bake for 15 minutes. 5. When completely cooked, a toothpick inserted in center will come out mostly clean. Serve warm.

● CHAPTER 2 Family Favorites

Scallops with Green Vegetables

Preparation time: 15 minutes | Cook time: 8 to 11 minutes | Serves 4

- ➢ 1 cup green beans
- ➢ 1 cup frozen peas
- ➢ 1 cup frozen chopped broccoli
- ➢ 2 teaspoons olive oil
- ➢ ½ teaspoon dried basil
- ➢ ½ teaspoon dried oregano
- ➢ 12 ounces (340 g) sea scallops

Instructions

1. In a large bowl, toss the green beans, peas, and broccoli with the olive oil. Place in the air fryer basket. Air fry at 400°F (204°C) for 4 to 6 minutes, or until the vegetables are crisp-tender. 2. Remove the vegetables from the air fryer basket and sprinkle with the herbs. Set aside. 3. In the air fryer basket, put the scallops and air fry for 4 to 5 minutes, or until the scallops are firm and reach an internal temperature of just 145°F (63°C) on a meat thermometer. 4. Toss scallops with the vegetables and serve immediately.

Pork Stuffing Meatballs

Preparation time: 10 minutes | Cook time: 12 minutes | Makes 35 meatballs

- ➢ Oil, for spraying
- ➢ 1½ pounds (680 g) ground pork
- ➢ 1 cup bread crumbs
- ➢ ½ cup milk
- ➢ ¼ cup minced onion
- ➢ 1 large egg
- ➢ 1 tablespoon dried rosemary
- ➢ 1 tablespoon dried thyme
- ➢ 1 teaspoon salt
- ➢ 1 teaspoon freshly ground black pepper
- ➢ 1 teaspoon finely chopped fresh parsley

Instructions

1. Line the air fryer basket with parchment and spray lightly with oil. 2. In a large bowl, mix together the ground pork, bread crumbs, milk, onion, egg, rosemary, thyme, salt, black pepper, and parsley. 3. Roll about 2 tablespoons of the mixture into a ball. Repeat with the rest of the mixture. You should have 30 to 35 meatballs. 4. Place the meatballs in the prepared basket in a single layer, leaving space between each one. You may need to work in batches, depending on the size of your air fryer. 5. Air fry at 390°F (199°C) for 10 to 12 minutes, flipping after 5 minutes, or until golden brown and the internal temperature reaches 160°F (71°C).

Veggie Tuna Melts

Preparation time: 15 minutes | Cook time: 7 to 11 minutes | Serves 4

- ➢ 2 low-sodium whole-wheat English muffins, split
- ➢ 1 (6 ounces / 170 g) can chunk light low-sodium tuna, drained
- ➢ 1 cup shredded carrot
- ➢ ⅓ cup chopped mushrooms
- ➢ 2 scallions, white and green parts, sliced
- ➢ ⅓ cup nonfat Greek yogurt
- ➢ 2 tablespoons low-sodium stone ground mustard
- ➢ 2 slices low-sodium low-fat Swiss cheese, halved

Instructions

1. Place the English muffin halves in the air fryer basket. Air fry at 340°F (171°C) for 3 to 4 minutes, or until crisp. Remove from the basket and set aside. 2. In a medium bowl, thoroughly mix the tuna, carrot, mushrooms, scallions, yogurt, and mustard. Top each half of the muffins with one-fourth of the tuna mixture and a half slice of Swiss cheese. 3. Air fry for 4 to 7 minutes, or until the tuna mixture is hot and the cheese melts and starts to brown. Serve immediately.

Fish and Vegetable Tacos

Preparation time: 15 minutes | Cook time: 9 to 12 minutes | Serves 4

- 1 pound (454 g) white fish fillets, such as sole or cod
- 2 teaspoons olive oil
- 3 tablespoons freshly squeezed lemon juice, divided
- 1½ cups chopped red cabbage
- 1 large carrot, grated
- ½ cup low-sodium salsa
- ⅓ cup low-fat Greek yogurt
- 4 soft low-sodium whole-wheat tortillas

Instructions

1. Brush the fish with the olive oil and sprinkle with 1 -tablespoon of lemon juice. Air fry in the air fryer basket at 390°F (199°C) for 9 to 12 minutes, or until the fish just flakes when tested with a fork. 2. Meanwhile, in a medium bowl, stir together the remaining 2 tablespoons of lemon juice, the red cabbage, carrot, salsa, and yogurt. 3. When the fish is cooked, remove it from the air fryer basket and break it up into large pieces. 4. Offer the fish, tortillas, and the cabbage mixture, and let each person assemble a taco.

Coconut Chicken Tenders

Preparation time: 10 minutes | Cook time: 12 minutes | Serves 4

- Oil, for spraying
- 2 large eggs
- ¼ cup milk
- 1 tablespoon hot sauce
- 1½ cups sweetened flaked coconut
- ¾ cup panko bread crumbs
- 1 teaspoon salt
- ½ teaspoon freshly ground black pepper
- 1 pound (454 g) chicken tenders

Instructions

1. Line the air fryer basket with parchment and spray lightly with oil. 2. In a small bowl, whisk together the eggs, milk, and hot sauce. 3. In a shallow dish, mix together the coconut, bread crumbs, salt, and black pepper. 4. Coat the chicken in the egg mix, then dredge in the coconut mixture until evenly coated. 5. Place the chicken in the prepared basket and spray liberally with oil. 6. Air fry at 400°F (204°C) for 6 minutes, flip, spray with more oil, and cook for another 6 minutes, or until the internal temperature reaches 165°F (74°C).

Berry Cheesecake

Preparation time: 5 minutes | Cook time: 10 minutes | Serves 4

- Oil, for spraying
- 8 ounces (227 g) cream cheese
- 6 tablespoons sugar
- 1 tablespoon sour cream
- 1 large egg
- ½ teaspoon vanilla extract
- ¼ teaspoon lemon juice
- ½ cup fresh mixed berries

Instructions

1. Preheat the air fryer to 350°F (177°C). Line the air fryer basket with parchment and spray lightly with oil. 2. In a blender, combine the cream cheese, sugar, sour cream, egg, vanilla, and lemon juice and blend until smooth. Pour the mixture into a 4-inch springform pan. 3. Place the pan in the prepared basket. 4. Cook for 8 to 10 minutes, or until only the very center jiggles slightly when the pan is moved. 5. Refrigerate the cheesecake in the pan for at least 2 hours. 6. Release the sides from the springform pan, top the cheesecake with the mixed berries, and serve.

Cajun Shrimp

Preparation time: 15 minutes | Cook time: 9 minutes | Serves 4

- Oil, for spraying
- 1 pound (454 g) jumbo raw shrimp, peeled and deveined
- 1 tablespoon Cajun seasoning
- 6 ounces (170 g) cooked kielbasa, cut into thick slices
- ½ medium zucchini, cut into ¼-inch-thick slices
- ½ medium yellow squash, cut into ¼-inch-thick slices
- 1 green bell pepper, seeded and cut into

1-inch pieces

➢ 2 tablespoons olive oil

➢ ½ teaspoon salt

Instructions

1. Preheat the air fryer to 400°F (204°C). Line the air fryer basket with parchment and spray lightly with oil. 2. In a large bowl, toss together the shrimp and Cajun seasoning. Add the kielbasa, zucchini, squash, bell pepper, olive oil, and salt and mix well. 3. Transfer the mixture to the prepared basket, taking care not to overcrowd. You may need to work in batches, depending on the size of your air fryer. 4. Cook for 9 minutes, shaking and stirring every 3 minutes. Serve immediately.

Churro Bites

Preparation time: 5 minutes | Cook time: 6 minutes | Makes 36 bites

➢ Oil, for spraying

➢ 1 (17¼ ounces / 489 g) package frozen puffed pastry, thawed

➢ 1 cup granulated sugar

➢ 1 tablespoon ground cinnamon

➢ ½ cup confectioners' sugar

➢ 1 tablespoon milk

Instructions

1. Preheat the air fryer to 400°F (204°C). Line the air fryer basket with parchment and spray lightly with oil. 2. Unfold the puff pastry onto a clean work surface. Using a sharp knife, cut the dough into 36 bite-size pieces. 3. Place the dough pieces in one layer in the prepared basket, taking care not to let the pieces touch or overlap. 4. Cook for 3 minutes, flip, and cook for another 3 minutes, or until puffed and golden. 5. In a small bowl, mix together the granulated sugar and cinnamon. 6. In another small bowl, whisk together the confectioners' sugar and milk. 7. Dredge the bites in the cinnamon-sugar mixture until evenly coated. 8. Serve with the icing on the side for dipping.

Bacon-Wrapped Hot Dogs

Preparation time: 5 minutes | Cook time: 10 minutes | Serves 4

➢ Oil, for spraying

➢ 4 bacon slices

➢ 4 all-beef hot dogs

➢ 4 hot dog buns

➢ Toppings of choice

Instructions

1. Line the air fryer basket with parchment and spray lightly with oil. 2. Wrap a strip of bacon tightly around each hot dog, taking care to cover the tips so they don't get too crispy. Secure with a toothpick at each end to keep the bacon from shrinking. 3. Place the hot dogs in the prepared basket. 4. Air fry at 380°F (193°C) for 8 to 9 minutes, depending on how crispy you like the bacon. For extra-crispy, cook the hot dogs at 400°F (204°C) for 6 to 8 minutes. 5. Place the hot dogs in the buns, return them to the air fryer, and cook for another 1 to 2 minutes, or until the buns are warm. Add your desired toppings and serve.

Cheesy Roasted Sweet Potatoes

Preparation time: 7 minutes | Cook time: 18 to 23 minutes | Serves 4

➢ 2 large sweet potatoes, peeled and sliced

➢ 1 teaspoon olive oil

➢ 1 tablespoon white balsamic vinegar

➢ 1 teaspoon dried thyme

➢ ¼ cup grated Parmesan cheese

Instructions

1. In a large bowl, drizzle the sweet potato slices with the olive oil and toss. 2. Sprinkle with the balsamic vinegar and thyme and toss again. 3. Sprinkle the potatoes with the Parmesan cheese and toss to coat. 4. Roast the slices, in batches, in the air fryer basket at 400°F (204°C) for 18 to 23 minutes, tossing the sweet potato slices in the basket once during cooking, until tender. 5. Repeat with the remaining sweet potato slices. Serve immediately.

Beef Jerky

Preparation time: 30 minutes | Cook time: 2 hours | Serves 8

➢ Oil, for spraying

➢ 1 pound (454 g) round steak, cut into thin, short slices

➢ ¼ cup soy sauce

- ➤ 3 tablespoons packed light brown sugar
- ➤ 1 tablespoon minced garlic
- ➤ 1 teaspoon ground ginger
- ➤ 1 tablespoon water

Instructions

1. Line the air fryer basket with parchment and spray lightly with oil. 2. Place the steak, soy sauce, brown sugar, garlic, ginger, and water in a zip-top plastic bag, seal, and shake well until evenly coated. Refrigerate for 30 minutes. 3. Place the steak in the prepared basket in a single layer. You may need to work in batches, depending on the size of your air fryer. 4. Air fry at 180°F (82°C) for at least 2 hours. Add more time if you like your jerky a bit tougher.

Phyllo Vegetable Triangles

Preparation time: 15 minutes | Cook time: 6 to 11 minutes | Serves 6

- ➤ 3 tablespoons minced onion
- ➤ 2 garlic cloves, minced
- ➤ 2 tablespoons grated carrot
- ➤ 1 teaspoon olive oil
- ➤ 3 tablespoons frozen baby peas, thawed
- ➤ 2 tablespoons nonfat cream cheese, at room temperature
- ➤ 6 sheets frozen phyllo dough, thawed
- ➤ Olive oil spray, for coating the dough

Instructions

1. In a baking pan, combine the onion, garlic, carrot, and olive oil. Air fry at 390°F (199°C) for 2 to 4 minutes, or until the vegetables are crisp-tender. Transfer to a bowl. 2. Stir in the peas and cream cheese to the vegetable mixture. Let cool while you prepare the dough. 3. Lay one sheet of phyllo on a work surface and lightly spray with olive oil spray. Top with another sheet of phyllo. Repeat with the remaining 4 phyllo sheets; you'll have 3 stacks with 2 layers each. Cut each stack lengthwise into 4 strips (12 strips total). 4. Place a scant 2 teaspoons of the filling near the bottom of each strip. Bring one corner up over the filling to make a triangle; continue folding the triangles over, as you would fold a flag. Seal the edge with a bit of water. Repeat with the remaining strips and filling. 5. Air fry the triangles, in 2 batches, for 4 to 7 minutes, or until golden brown. Serve.

Apple Pie Egg Rolls

Preparation time: 10 minutes | Cook time: 8 minutes | Makes 6 rolls

- ➤ Oil, for spraying
- ➤ 1 (21 ounces / 595 g) can apple pie filling
- ➤ 1 tablespoon all-purpose flour
- ➤ ½ teaspoon lemon juice
- ➤ ¼ teaspoon ground nutmeg
- ➤ ¼ teaspoon ground cinnamon
- ➤ 6 egg roll wrappers

Instructions

1. Preheat the air fryer to 400°F (204°C). Line the air fryer basket with parchment and spray lightly with oil. 2. In a medium bowl, mix together the pie filling, flour, lemon juice, nutmeg, and cinnamon. 3. Lay out the egg roll wrappers on a work surface and spoon a dollop of pie filling in the center of each. 4. Fill a small bowl with water. Dip your finger in the water and, working one at a time, moisten the edges of the wrappers. Fold the wrapper like an envelope: First fold one corner into the center. Fold each side corner in, and then fold over the remaining corner, making sure each corner overlaps a bit and the moistened edges stay closed. Use additional water and your fingers to seal any open edges. 5. Place the rolls in the prepared basket and spray liberally with oil. You may need to work in batches, depending on the size of your air fryer. 6. Cook for 4 minutes, flip, spray with oil, and cook for another 4 minutes, or until crispy and golden brown. Serve immediately.

Mixed Berry Crumble

Preparation time: 10 minutes | Cook time: 11 to 16 minutes | Serves 4

- ➤ ½ cup chopped fresh strawberries
- ➤ ½ cup fresh blueberries
- ➤ ⅓ cup frozen raspberries
- ➤ 1 tablespoon freshly squeezed lemon juice
- ➤ 1 tablespoon honey
- ➤ ⅔ cup whole-wheat pastry flour
- ➤ 3 tablespoons packed brown sugar

> 2 tablespoons unsalted butter, melted

Instructions

1. In a baking pan, combine the strawberries, blue-berries, and raspberries. Drizzle with the lemon juice and honey. 2. In a small bowl, mix the pastry flour and brown sugar. 3. Stir in the butter and mix until crumbly. Sprinkle this mixture over the fruit. 4. Bake at 380°F (193°C) for 11 to 16 minutes, or until the fruit is tender and bubbly and the topping is golden brown. Serve warm.

Old Bay Tilapia

Preparation time: 15 minutes | Cook time: 6 minutes | Serves 4

> Oil, for spraying
> 1 cup panko bread crumbs
> 2 tablespoons Old Bay seasoning
> 2 teaspoons granulated garlic
> 1 teaspoon onion powder
> ½ teaspoon salt
> ¼ teaspoon freshly ground black pepper
> 1 large egg
> 4 tilapia fillets

Instructions

1. Preheat the air fryer to 400°F (204°C). Line the air fryer basket with parchment and spray lightly with oil. 2. In a shallow bowl, mix together the bread crumbs, Old Bay, garlic, onion powder, salt, and black pepper. 3. In a small bowl, whisk the egg. 4. Coat the tilapia in the egg, then dredge in the bread crumb mixture until completely coated. 5. Place the tilapia in the prepared basket. You may need to work in batches, depending on the size of your air fryer. Spray lightly with oil. 6. Cook for 4 to 6 minutes,

depending on the thickness of the fillets, until the internal temperature reaches 145°F (63°C). Serve immediately.

Puffed Egg Tarts

Preparation time: 10 minutes | Cook time: 42 minutes | Makes 4 tarts

> Oil, for spraying
> All-purpose flour, for dusting
> 1 (12 ounces / 340 g) sheet frozen puff pastry, thawed
> ¾ cup shredded Cheddar cheese, divided
> 4 large eggs
> 2 teaspoons chopped fresh parsley
> Salt and freshly ground black pepper, to taste

Instructions

1. Preheat the air fryer to 390°F (199°C). Line the air fryer basket with parchment and spray lightly with oil. 2. Lightly dust your work surface with flour. Unfold the puff pastry and cut it into 4 equal squares. Place 2 squares in the prepared basket. 3. Cook for 10 minutes. 4. Remove the basket. Press the center of each tart shell with a spoon to make an indentation. 5. Sprinkle 3 tablespoons of cheese into each indentation and crack 1 egg into the center of each tart shell. 6. Cook for another 7 to 11 minutes, or until the eggs are cooked to your desired doneness. 7. Repeat with the remaining puff pastry squares, cheese, and eggs. 8. Sprinkle evenly with the parsley, and season with salt and black pepper. Serve immediately.

● CHAPTER 3 Tasty Everyday Favorites

Cheesy Chile Toast

Preparation time: 5 minutes | Cook time: 5 minutes | Serves 1

- 2 tablespoons grated Parmesan cheese
- 2 tablespoons grated Mozzarella cheese
- 2 teaspoons salted butter, at room temperature
- 10 to 15 thin slices serrano chile or jalapeño
- 2 slices sourdough bread
- ½ teaspoon black pepper

Instructions

1. Preheat the air fryer to 325°F (163°C). 2. In a small bowl, stir together the Parmesan, Mozzarella, butter, and chiles. 3. Spread half the mixture onto one side of each slice of bread. Sprinkle with the pepper. Place the slices, cheese-side up, in the air fryer basket. Bake for 5 minutes, or until the cheese has melted and started to brown slightly. 4. Serve immediately.

Bacon Pinwheels

Preparation time: 10 minutes | Cook time: 10 minutes | Makes 8 pinwheels

- 1 sheet puff pastry
- 2 tablespoons maple syrup
- ¼ cup brown sugar
- 8 slices bacon
- Ground black pepper, to taste
- Cooking spray

Instructions

1. Preheat the air fryer to 360°F (182°C). Spritz the air fryer basket with cooking spray. 2. Roll the puff pastry into a 10-inch square with a rolling pin on a clean work surface, then cut the pastry into 8 strips. 3. Brush the strips with maple syrup and sprinkle with sugar, leaving a 1-inch far end uncovered. 4. Arrange each slice of bacon on each strip, leaving a ⅛-inch length of bacon hang over the end close to

you. Sprinkle with black pepper. 5. From the end close to you, roll the strips into pinwheels, then dab the uncovered end with water and seal the rolls. 6. Arrange the pinwheels in the preheated air fryer and spritz with cooking spray. 7. Air fry for 10 minutes or until golden brown. Flip the pinwheels halfway through. 8. Serve immediately.

Buttery Sweet Potatoes

Preparation time: 5 minutes | Cook time: 10 minutes | Serves 4

- 2 tablespoons butter, melted
- 1 tablespoon light brown sugar
- 2 sweet potatoes, peeled and cut into ½-inch cubes
- Cooking spray

Instructions

1. Preheat the air fryer to 400°F (204°C). Line the air fryer basket with parchment paper. 2. In a medium bowl, stir together the melted butter and brown sugar until blended. Toss the sweet potatoes in the butter mixture until coated. 3. Place the sweet potatoes on the parchment and spritz with oil. 4. Air fry for 5 minutes. Shake the basket, spritz the sweet potatoes with oil, and air fry for 5 minutes more until they're soft enough to cut with a fork. 5. Serve immediately.

Easy Cinnamon Toast

Preparation time: 5 minutes | Cook time: 20 minutes | Serves 6

- 1½ teaspoons cinnamon
- 1½ teaspoons vanilla extract
- ½ cup sugar
- 2 teaspoons ground black pepper
- 2 tablespoons melted coconut oil
- 12 slices whole wheat bread

Instructions

1. Preheat the air fryer to 400°F (204°C). 2. Combine all the ingredients, except for the bread, in

a large bowl. Stir to mix well. 3. Dunk the bread in the bowl of mixture gently to coat and infuse well. Shake the excess off. 4. Arrange the bread slices in the preheated air fryer. Air fry for 5 minutes or until golden brown. Flip the bread halfway through. You may need to cook in batches to avoid overcrowding. 5. Remove the bread slices from the air fryer and slice to serve.

Simple Pea Delight

Preparation time: 5 minutes | Cook time: 15 minutes | Serves 2 to 4

➢ 1 cup flour
➢ 1 teaspoon baking powder
➢ 3 eggs
➢ 1 cup coconut milk
➢ 1 cup cream cheese
➢ 3 tablespoons pea protein
➢ ½ cup chicken or turkey strips
➢ Pinch of sea salt
➢ 1 cup Mozzarella cheese

Instructions

1. Preheat the air fryer to 390°F (199°C). 2. In a large bowl, mix all ingredients together using a large wooden spoon. 3. Spoon equal amounts of the mixture into muffin cups and bake for 15 minutes. 4. Serve immediately.

Scalloped Veggie Mix

Preparation time: 10 minutes | Cook time: 15 minutes | Serves 4

➢ 1 Yukon Gold potato, thinly sliced
➢ 1 small sweet potato, peeled and thinly sliced
➢ 1 medium carrot, thinly sliced
➢ ¼ cup minced onion
➢ 3 garlic cloves, minced
➢ ¾ cup 2 percent milk
➢ 2 tablespoons cornstarch
➢ ½ teaspoon dried thyme

Instructions

1. Preheat the air fryer to 380°F (193°C). 2. In a baking pan, layer the potato, sweet potato, carrot, onion, and garlic. 3. In a small bowl, whisk the milk, cornstarch, and thyme until blended. Pour the milk

mixture evenly over the vegetables in the pan. 4. Bake for 15 minutes. Check the casserole—it should be golden brown on top, and the vegetables should be tender. 5. Serve immediately.

Air Fried Zucchini Sticks

Preparation time: 5 minutes | Cook time: 20 minutes | Serves 4

➢ 1 medium zucchini, cut into 48 sticks
➢ ¼ cup seasoned breadcrumbs
➢ 1 tablespoon melted buttery spread
➢ Cooking spray

Instructions

1. Preheat the air fryer to 360°F (182°C). Spritz the air fryer basket with cooking spray and set aside. 2. In 2 different shallow bowls, add the seasoned breadcrumbs and the buttery spread. 3. One by one, dredge the zucchini sticks into the buttery spread, then roll in the breadcrumbs to coat evenly. Arrange the crusted sticks on a plate. 4. Place the zucchini sticks in the prepared air fryer basket. Work in two batches to avoid overcrowding. 5. Air fry for 10 minutes, or until golden brown and crispy. Shake the basket halfway through to cook evenly. 6. When the cooking time is over, transfer the fries to a wire rack. Rest for 5 minutes and serve warm.

Air Fried Shishito Peppers

Preparation time: 5 minutes | Cook time: 5 minutes | Serves 4

➢ ½ pound (227 g) shishito peppers (about 24)
➢ 1 tablespoon olive oil
➢ Coarse sea salt, to taste
➢ Lemon wedges, for serving
➢ Cooking spray

Instructions

1. Preheat the air fryer to 400°F (204°C). Spritz the air fryer basket with cooking spray. 2. Toss the peppers with olive oil in a large bowl to coat well. 3. Arrange the peppers in the preheated air fryer. 4. Air fryer for 5 minutes or until blistered and lightly charred. Shake the basket and sprinkle the peppers with salt halfway through the cooking time. 5. Transfer the peppers onto a plate and squeeze the

lemon wedges on top before serving.

Cheesy Potato Patties

Preparation time: 5 minutes | Cook time: 10 minutes | Serves 8

- ➤ 2 pounds (907 g) white potatoes
- ➤ ½ cup finely chopped scallions
- ➤ ½ teaspoon freshly ground black pepper, or more to taste
- ➤ 1 tablespoon fine sea salt
- ➤ ½ teaspoon hot paprika
- ➤ 2 cups shredded Colby cheese
- ➤ ¼ cup canola oil
- ➤ 1 cup crushed crackers

Instructions

1. Preheat the air fryer to 360°F (182°C). 2. Boil the potatoes until soft. Dry them off and peel them before mashing thoroughly, leaving no lumps. 3. Combine the mashed potatoes with scallions, pepper, salt, paprika, and cheese. 4. Mold the mixture into balls with your hands and press with your palm to flatten them into patties. 5. In a shallow dish, combine the canola oil and crushed crackers. Coat the patties in the crumb mixture. 6. Bake the patties for about 10 minutes, in multiple batches if necessary. 7. Serve hot.

Spicy Air Fried Old Bay Shrimp

Preparation time: 7 minutes | Cook time: 10 minutes | Makes 2 cups

- ➤ ½ teaspoon Old Bay Seasoning
- ➤ 1 teaspoon ground cayenne pepper
- ➤ ½ teaspoon paprika
- ➤ 1 tablespoon olive oil
- ➤ ⅛ teaspoon salt
- ➤ ½ pound (227 g) shrimps, peeled and deveined
- ➤ Juice of half a lemon

Instructions

1. Preheat the air fryer to 390°F (199°C). 2. Combine the Old Bay Seasoning, cayenne pepper, paprika, olive oil, and salt in a large bowl, then add the shrimps and toss to coat well. 3. Put the shrimps in the preheated air fryer. Air fry for 10 minutes or until opaque. Flip the shrimps halfway through. 4. Serve

the shrimps with lemon juice on top.

Crispy Potato Chips with Lemony Cream Dip

Preparation time: 20 minutes | Cook time: 15 minutes | Serves 2 to 4

- ➤ 2 large russet potatoes, sliced into ⅛-inch slices, rinsed
- ➤ Sea salt and freshly ground black pepper, to taste
- ➤ Cooking spray
- ➤ Lemony Cream Dip:
- ➤ ½ cup sour cream
- ➤ ¼ teaspoon lemon juice
- ➤ 2 scallions, white part only, minced
- ➤ 1 tablespoon olive oil
- ➤ ¼ teaspoon salt
- ➤ Freshly ground black pepper, to taste

Instructions

1. Soak the potato slices in water for 10 minutes, then pat dry with paper towels. 2. Preheat the air fryer to 300°F (149°C). 3. Transfer the potato slices in the preheated air fryer. Spritz the slices with cooking spray. You may need to work in batches to avoid overcrowding. 4. Air fry for 15 minutes or until crispy and golden brown. Shake the basket periodically. Sprinkle with salt and ground black pepper in the last minute. 5. Meanwhile, combine the ingredients for the dip in a small bowl. Stir to mix well. 6. Serve the potato chips immediately with the dip.

Herb-Roasted Veggies

Preparation time: 10 minutes | Cook time: 14 to 18 minutes | Serves 4

- ➤ 1 red bell pepper, sliced
- ➤ 1 (8 ounces / 227 g) package sliced mushrooms
- ➤ 1 cup green beans, cut into 2-inch pieces
- ➤ ⅓ cup diced red onion
- ➤ 3 garlic cloves, sliced
- ➤ 1 teaspoon olive oil
- ➤ ½ teaspoon dried basil
- ➤ ½ teaspoon dried tarragon

Instructions

1. Preheat the air fryer to 350°F (177°C). 2. In a medium bowl, mix the red bell pepper, mushrooms, green beans, red onion, and garlic. Drizzle with the olive oil. Toss to coat. 3. Add the herbs and toss again. 4. Place the vegetables in the air fryer basket. Roast for 14 to 18 minutes, or until tender. Serve immediately.

Easy Devils on Horseback

Preparation time: 5 minutes | Cook time: 7 minutes | Serves 12

➢ 24 petite pitted prunes (4½ ounces / 128 g)
➢ ¼ cup crumbled blue cheese, divided
➢ 8 slices center-cut bacon, cut crosswise into thirds

Instructions

1. Preheat the air fryer to 400°F (204°C). 2. Halve the prunes lengthwise, but don't cut them all the way through. Place ½ teaspoon of cheese in the center of each prune. Wrap a piece of bacon around each prune and secure the bacon with a toothpick. 3. Working in batches, arrange a single layer of the prunes in the air fryer basket. Air fry for about 7 minutes, flipping halfway, until the bacon is cooked through and crisp. 4. Let cool slightly and serve warm.

Crispy Green Tomatoes Slices

Preparation time: 10 minutes | Cook time: 8 minutes | Makes 12 slices

➢ ½ cup all-purpose flour
➢ 1 egg
➢ ½ cup buttermilk
➢ 1 cup cornmeal
➢ 1 cup panko
➢ 2 green tomatoes, cut into ¼-inch-thick slices, patted dry
➢ ½ teaspoon salt
➢ ½ teaspoon ground black pepper
➢ Cooking spray

Instructions

1. Preheat the air fryer to 400°F (204°C). Line the air fryer basket with parchment paper. 2. Pour the flour in a bowl. Whisk the egg and buttermilk in a second bowl. Combine the cornmeal and panko in a third bowl. 3. Dredge the tomato slices in the bowl of flour first, then into the egg mixture, and then dunk the slices into the cornmeal mixture. Shake the excess off. 4. Transfer the well-coated tomato slices in the preheated air fryer and sprinkle with salt and ground black pepper. 5. Spritz the tomato slices with cooking spray. Air fry for 8 minutes or until crispy and lightly browned. Flip the slices halfway through the cooking time. 6. Serve immediately.

Easy Roasted Asparagus

Preparation time: 5 minutes | Cook time: 6 minutes | Serves 4

➢ 1 pound (454 g) asparagus, trimmed and halved crosswise
➢ 1 teaspoon extra-virgin olive oil
➢ Salt and pepper, to taste
➢ Lemon wedges, for serving

Instructions

1. Preheat the air fryer to 400°F (204°C). 2. Toss the asparagus with the oil, ⅛ teaspoon salt, and ⅛ teaspoon pepper in bowl. Transfer to air fryer basket. 3. Place the basket in air fryer and roast for 6 to 8 minutes, or until tender and bright green, tossing halfway through cooking. 4. Season with salt and pepper and serve with lemon wedges.

Corn Fritters

Preparation time: 15 minutes | Cook time: 8 minutes | Serves 6

➢ 1 cup self-rising flour
➢ 1 tablespoon sugar
➢ 1 teaspoon salt
➢ 1 large egg, lightly beaten
➢ ¼ cup buttermilk
➢ ¾ cup corn kernels
➢ ¼ cup minced onion
➢ Cooking spray

Instructions

1. Preheat the air fryer to 350°F (177°C). Line the air fryer basket with parchment paper. 2. In a medium bowl, whisk the flour, sugar, and salt until blended. Stir in the egg and buttermilk. Add the corn and minced onion. Mix well. Shape the corn fritter batter

into 12 balls. 3. Place the fritters on the parchment and spritz with oil. Bake for 4 minutes. Flip the fritters, spritz them with oil, and bake for 4 minutes more until firm and lightly browned. 4. Serve immediately.

Beef Bratwursts

Preparation time: 5 minutes | Cook time: 15 minutes | Serves 4

➢ 4 (3-ounce / 85-g) beef bratwursts

Instructions

1. Preheat the air fryer to 375ºF (191ºC). 2. Place the beef bratwursts in the air fryer basket and air fry for 15 minutes, turning once halfway through. 3. Serve hot.

Indian-Style Sweet Potato Fries

Preparation time: 5 minutes | Cook time: 8 minutes | Makes 20 fries

➢ Seasoning Mixture:
➢ ¾ teaspoon ground coriander
➢ ½ teaspoon garam masala
➢ ½ teaspoon garlic powder
➢ ½ teaspoon ground cumin
➢ ¼ teaspoon ground cayenne pepper
➢ Fries:
➢ 2 large sweet potatoes, peeled
➢ 2 teaspoons olive oil

Instructions

1. Preheat the air fryer to 400ºF (204ºC). 2. In a small bowl, combine the coriander, garam masala, garlic powder, cumin, and cayenne pepper. 3. Slice the sweet potatoes into ¼-inch-thick fries. 4. In a large bowl, toss the sliced sweet potatoes with the olive oil and the seasoning mixture. 5. Transfer the seasoned sweet potatoes to the air fryer basket and fry for 8 minutes, until crispy. 6. Serve warm.

● CHAPTER 4 Poultry and Meat

Greek Chicken Stir-Fry

Preparation time: 15 minutes | Cook time: 15 minutes | Serves 2

➢ 1 (6-ounce / 170-g) chicken breast, cut into 1-inch cubes
➢ ½ medium zucchini, chopped
➢ ½ medium red bell pepper, seeded and chopped
➢ ¼ medium red onion, peeled and sliced
➢ 1 tablespoon coconut oil
➢ 1 teaspoon dried oregano
➢ ½ teaspoon garlic powder
➢ ¼ teaspoon dried thyme

Instructions

1. Place all ingredients into a large mixing bowl and toss until the coconut oil coats the meat and vegetables. Pour the contents of the bowl into the air fryer basket. 2. Adjust the temperature to 375°F (191°C) and air fry for 15 minutes. 3. Shake the basket halfway through the cooking time to redistribute the food. Serve immediately.

Crisp Paprika Chicken Drumsticks

Preparation time: 5 minutes | Cook time: 22 minutes | Serves 2

➢ 2 teaspoons paprika
➢ 1 teaspoon packed brown sugar
➢ 1 teaspoon garlic powder
➢ ½ teaspoon dry mustard
➢ ½ teaspoon salt
➢ Pinch pepper
➢ 4 (5 ounces / 142 g) chicken drumsticks, trimmed
➢ 1 teaspoon vegetable oil
➢ 1 scallion, green part only, sliced thin on bias

Instructions

1. Preheat the air fryer to 400°F (204°C). 2.

Combine paprika, sugar, garlic powder, mustard, salt, and pepper in a bowl. Pat drumsticks dry with paper towels. Using metal skewer, poke 10 to 15 holes in skin of each drumstick. Rub with oil and sprinkle evenly with spice mixture. 3. Arrange drumsticks in air fryer basket, spaced evenly apart, alternating ends. Air fry until chicken is crisp and registers 195°F (91°C), 22 to 25 minutes, flipping chicken halfway through cooking. 4. Transfer chicken to serving platter, tent loosely with aluminum foil, and let rest for 5 minutes. Sprinkle with scallion and serve.

Chicken Shawarma

Preparation time: 30 minutes | Cook time: 15 minutes | Serves 4

➢ Shawarma Spice:
➢ 2 teaspoons dried oregano
➢ 1 teaspoon ground cinnamon
➢ 1 teaspoon ground cumin
➢ 1 teaspoon ground coriander
➢ 1 teaspoon kosher salt
➢ ½ teaspoon ground allspice
➢ ½ teaspoon cayenne pepper
➢ Chicken:
➢ 1 pound (454 g) boneless, skinless chicken thighs, cut into large bite-size chunks
➢ 2 tablespoons vegetable oil
➢ For Serving:
➢ Tzatziki
➢ Pita bread

Instructions

1. For the shawarma spice: In a small bowl, combine the oregano, cayenne, cumin, coriander, salt, cinnamon, and allspice. 2. For the chicken: In a large bowl, toss together the chicken, vegetable oil, and shawarma spice to coat. Marinate at room temperature for 30 minutes or cover and refrigerate for up to 24 hours. 3. Place the chicken in the air

fryer basket. Set the air fryer to 350ºF (177ºC) for 15 minutes, or until the chicken reaches an internal temperature of 165ºF (74ºC). 4. Transfer the chicken to a serving platter. Serve with tzatziki and pita bread.

Chicken with Pineapple and Peach

Preparation time: 10 minutes | Cook time: 14 to 15 minutes | Serves 4

- ➢ 1 pound (454 g) low-sodium boneless, skinless chicken breasts, cut into 1-inch pieces
- ➢ 1 medium red onion, chopped
- ➢ 1 (8-ounce / 227-g) can pineapple chunks, drained, ¼ cup juice reserved
- ➢ 1 tablespoon peanut oil or safflower oil
- ➢ 1 peach, peeled, pitted, and cubed
- ➢ 1 tablespoon cornstarch
- ➢ ½ teaspoon ground ginger
- ➢ ¼ teaspoon ground allspice
- ➢ Brown rice, cooked (optional)

Instructions

1. Preheat the air fryer to 380ºF (193ºC). 2. In a medium metal bowl, mix the chicken, red onion, pineapple, and peanut oil. Bake in the air fryer for 9 minutes. Remove and stir. 3. Add the peach and return the bowl to the air fryer. Bake for 3 minutes more. Remove and stir again. 4. In a small bowl, whisk the reserved pineapple juice, the cornstarch, ginger, and allspice well. Add to the chicken mixture and stir to combine. 5. Bake for 2 to 3 minutes more, or until the chicken reaches an internal temperature of 165ºF (74ºC) on a meat thermometer and the sauce is slightly thickened. 6. Serve immediately over hot cooked brown rice, if desired.

Chicken Cordon Bleu

Preparation time: 20 minutes | Cook time: 15 to 20 minutes | Serves 4

- ➢ 4 small boneless, skinless chicken breasts
- ➢ Salt and pepper, to taste
- ➢ 4 slices deli ham

- ➢ 4 slices deli Swiss cheese (about 3 to 4 inches square)
- ➢ 2 tablespoons olive oil
- ➢ 2 teaspoons marjoram
- ➢ ¼ teaspoon paprika

Instructions

1. Split each chicken breast horizontally almost in two, leaving one edge intact. 2. Lay breasts open flat and sprinkle with salt and pepper to taste. 3. Place a ham slice on top of each chicken breast. 4. Cut cheese slices in half and place one half atop each breast. Set aside remaining halves of cheese slices. 5. Roll up chicken breasts to enclose cheese and ham and secure with toothpicks. 6. Mix together the olive oil, marjoram, and paprika. Rub all over outsides of chicken breasts. 7. Place chicken in air fryer basket and air fry at 360ºF (182ºC) for 15 to 20 minutes, until well done and juices run clear. 8. Remove all toothpicks. To avoid burns, place chicken breasts on a plate to remove toothpicks, then immediately return them to the air fryer basket. 9. Place a half cheese slice on top of each chicken breast and cook for a minute or so just to melt cheese.

Lemon Chicken

Preparation time: 5 minutes | Cook time: 20 to 25 minutes | Serves 4

- ➢ 8 bone-in chicken thighs, skin on
- ➢ 1 tablespoon olive oil
- ➢ 1½ teaspoons lemon-pepper seasoning
- ➢ ½ teaspoon paprika
- ➢ ½ teaspoon garlic powder
- ➢ ¼ teaspoon freshly ground black pepper
- ➢ Juice of ½ lemon

Instructions

1. Preheat the air fryer to 360ºF (182ºC). 2. Place the chicken in a large bowl and drizzle with the olive oil. Top with the lemon-pepper seasoning, paprika, garlic powder, and freshly ground black pepper. Toss until thoroughly coated. 3. Working in batches if necessary, arrange the chicken in a single layer in the basket of the air fryer. Pausing halfway through the cooking time to turn the chicken, air fry for 20 to 25 minutes, until a thermometer inserted into the

thickest piece registers 165°F (74°C). 4. Transfer the chicken to a serving platter and squeeze the lemon juice over the top.

Chicken Drumsticks with Barbecue-Honey Sauce

Preparation time: 5 minutes | Cook time: 40 minutes | Serves 5

- 1 tablespoon olive oil
- 10 chicken drumsticks
- Chicken seasoning or rub, to taste
- Salt and ground black pepper, to taste
- 1 cup barbecue sauce
- ¼ cup honey

Instructions

1. Preheat the air fryer to 390°F (199°C). Grease the air fryer basket with olive oil. 2. Rub the chicken drumsticks with chicken seasoning or rub, salt and ground black pepper on a clean work surface. 3. Arrange the chicken drumsticks in a single layer in the air fryer, then air fry for 18 minutes or until lightly browned. Flip the drumsticks halfway through. You may need to work in batches to avoid overcrowding. 4. Meanwhile, combine the barbecue sauce and honey in a small bowl. Stir to mix well. 5. Remove the drumsticks from the air fryer and baste with the sauce mixture to serve.

Apricot-Glazed Turkey Tenderloin

Preparation time: 20 minutes | Cook time: 30 minutes | Serves 4

- Olive oil
- ¼ cup sugar-free apricot preserves
- ½ tablespoon spicy brown mustard
- 1½ pounds (680 g) turkey breast tenderloin
- Salt and freshly ground black pepper, to taste

Instructions

1. Spray the air fryer basket lightly with olive oil. 2. In a small bowl, combine the apricot preserves and mustard to make a paste. 3. Season the turkey with salt and pepper. Spread the apricot paste all over the turkey. 4. Place the turkey in the air fryer basket and lightly spray with olive oil. 5. Air fry at 370°F (188°C) for 15 minutes. Flip the turkey over and lightly spray with olive oil. Air fry until the internal temperature reaches at least 170°F (77°C), an additional 10 to 15 minutes. 6. Let the turkey rest for 10 minutes before slicing and serving.

Garlic Parmesan Drumsticks

Preparation time: 5 minutes | Cook time: 25 minutes | Serves 4

- 8 (4-ounce / 113-g) chicken drumsticks
- ½ teaspoon salt
- ⅛ teaspoon ground black pepper
- ½ teaspoon garlic powder
- 2 tablespoons salted butter, melted
- ½ cup grated Parmesan cheese
- 1 tablespoon dried parsley

Instructions

1. Sprinkle drumsticks with salt, pepper, and garlic powder. Place drumsticks into ungreased air fryer basket. 2. Adjust the temperature to 400°F (204°C) and air fry for 25 minutes, turning drumsticks halfway through cooking. Drumsticks will be golden and have an internal temperature of at least 165°F (74°C) when done. 3. Transfer drumsticks to a large serving dish. Pour butter over drumsticks, and sprinkle with Parmesan and parsley. Serve warm.

Indian Fennel Chicken

Preparation time: 30 minutes | Cook time: 15 minutes | Serves 4

- 1 pound (454 g) boneless, skinless chicken thighs, cut crosswise into thirds
- 1 yellow onion, cut into 1½-inch-thick slices
- 1 tablespoon coconut oil, melted
- 2 teaspoons minced fresh ginger
- 2 teaspoons minced garlic
- 1 teaspoon smoked paprika
- 1 teaspoon ground fennel
- 1 teaspoon garam masala
- 1 teaspoon ground turmeric
- 1 teaspoon kosher salt
- ½ to 1 teaspoon cayenne pepper

- ➤ Vegetable oil spray
- ➤ 2 teaspoons fresh lemon juice
- ➤ ¼ cup chopped fresh cilantro or parsley

Instructions

1. Use a fork to pierce the chicken all over to allow the marinade to penetrate better. 2. In a large bowl, combine the onion, coconut oil, ginger, garlic, paprika, fennel, garam masala, turmeric, salt, and cayenne. Add the chicken, toss to combine, and marinate at room temperature for 30 minutes, or cover and refrigerate for up to 24 hours. 3. Place the chicken and onion in the air fryer basket. (Discard remaining marinade.) Spray with some vegetable oil spray. Set the air fryer to 350°F (177°C) for 15 minutes. Halfway through the cooking time, remove the basket, spray the chicken and onion with more vegetable oil spray, and toss gently to coat. At the end of the cooking time, use a meat thermometer to ensure the chicken has reached an internal temperature of 165°F (74°C). 4. Transfer the chicken and onion to a serving platter. Sprinkle with the lemon juice and cilantro and serve.

Tortilla Crusted Chicken Breast

Preparation time: 10 minutes | Cook time: 12 minutes | Serves 2

- ➤ ⅓ cup flour
- ➤ 1 teaspoon salt
- ➤ 1½ teaspoons chili powder
- ➤ 1 teaspoon ground cumin
- ➤ Freshly ground black pepper, to taste
- ➤ 1 egg, beaten
- ➤ ¾ cup coarsely crushed yellow corn tortilla chips
- ➤ 2 (3 to 4 ounces / 85 to 113 g) boneless chicken breasts
- ➤ Vegetable oil
- ➤ ½ cup salsa
- ➤ ½ cup crumbled queso fresco
- ➤ Fresh cilantro leaves
- ➤ Sour cream or guacamole (optional)

Instructions

1. Set up a dredging station with three shallow dishes. Combine the flour, salt, chili powder, cumin and black pepper in the first shallow dish. Beat the egg in the second shallow dish. Place the crushed tortilla chips in the third shallow dish. 2. Dredge the chicken in the spiced flour, covering all sides of the breast. Then dip the chicken into the egg, coating the chicken completely. Finally, place the chicken into the tortilla chips and press the chips onto the chicken to make sure they adhere to all sides of the breast. Spray the coated chicken breasts on both sides with vegetable oil. 3. Preheat the air fryer to 380°F (193°C). 4. Air fry the chicken for 6 minutes. Then turn the chicken breasts over and air fry for another 6 minutes. (Increase the cooking time if you are using chicken breasts larger than 3 to 4 ounces / 85 to 113 g.) 5. When the chicken has finished cooking, serve each breast with a little salsa, the crumbled queso fresco and cilantro as the finishing touch. Serve some sour cream and/or guacamole at the table, if desired.

Classic Whole Chicken

Preparation time: 5 minutes | Cook time: 50 minutes | Serves 4

- ➤ Oil, for spraying

1 (4-pound / Instructions

1.8-kg) whole chicken, giblets removed

- ➤ 1 tablespoon olive oil
- ➤ 1 teaspoon paprika
- ➤ ½ teaspoon granulated garlic
- ➤ ½ teaspoon salt
- ➤ ½ teaspoon freshly ground black pepper
- ➤ ¼ teaspoon finely chopped fresh parsley, for garnish

Instructions

1. Line the air fryer basket with parchment and spray lightly with oil. 2. Pat the chicken dry with paper towels. Rub it with the olive oil until evenly coated. 3. In a small bowl, mix together the paprika, garlic, salt, and black pepper and sprinkle it evenly over the chicken. 4. Place the chicken in the prepared basket, breast-side down. 5. Air fry at 360°F (182°C) for 30 minutes, flip, and cook for another 20 minutes, or until the internal temperature reaches 165°F (74°C) and the juices run clear. 6. Sprinkle with the parsley

before serving.

Coconut Chicken Meatballs

Preparation time: 10 minutes | Cook time: 14 minutes | Serves 4

- ➢ 1 pound (454 g) ground chicken
- ➢ 2 scallions, finely chopped
- ➢ 1 cup chopped fresh cilantro leaves
- ➢ ¼ cup unsweetened shredded coconut
- ➢ 1 tablespoon hoisin sauce
- ➢ 1 tablespoon soy sauce
- ➢ 2 teaspoons Sriracha or other hot sauce
- ➢ 1 teaspoon toasted sesame oil
- ➢ ½ teaspoon kosher salt
- ➢ 1 teaspoon black pepper

Instructions

1. In a large bowl, gently mix the chicken, scallions, cilantro, coconut, hoisin, soy sauce, Sriracha, sesame oil, salt, and pepper until thoroughly combined (the mixture will be wet and sticky). 2. Place a sheet of parchment paper in the air fryer basket. Using a small scoop or teaspoon, drop rounds of the mixture in a single layer onto the parchment paper. 3. Set the air fryer to 350°F (177°C) for 10 minutes, turning the meatballs halfway through the cooking time. Raise the air fryer temperature to 400°F (204°C) and cook for 4 minutes more to brown the outsides of the meatballs. Use a meat thermometer to ensure the meatballs have reached an internal temperature of 165°F (74°C). 4. Transfer the meatballs to a serving platter. Repeat with any remaining chicken mixture.

Fajita-Stuffed Chicken Breast

Preparation time: 15 minutes | Cook time: 25 minutes | Serves 4

- ➢ 2 (6-ounce / 170-g) boneless, skinless chicken breasts
- ➢ ¼ medium white onion, peeled and sliced
- ➢ 1 medium green bell pepper, seeded and sliced
- ➢ 1 tablespoon coconut oil
- ➢ 2 teaspoons chili powder
- ➢ 1 teaspoon ground cumin
- ➢ ½ teaspoon garlic powder

Instructions

1. Slice each chicken breast completely in half lengthwise into two even pieces. Using a meat tenderizer, pound out the chicken until it's about ¼-inch thickness. 2. Lay each slice of chicken out and place three slices of onion and four slices of green pepper on the end closest to you. Begin rolling the peppers and onions tightly into the chicken. Secure the roll with either toothpicks or a couple pieces of butcher's twine. 3. Drizzle coconut oil over chicken. Sprinkle each side with chili powder, cumin, and garlic powder. Place each roll into the air fryer basket. 4. Adjust the temperature to 350°F (177°C) and air fry for 25 minutes. 5. Serve warm.

Chicken Burgers with Ham and Cheese

Preparation time: 12 minutes | Cook time: 13 to 16 minutes | Serves 4

- ➢ ⅓ cup soft bread crumbs
- ➢ 3 tablespoons milk
- ➢ 1 egg, beaten
- ➢ ½ teaspoon dried thyme
- ➢ Pinch salt
- ➢ Freshly ground black pepper, to taste
- ➢ 1¼ pounds (567 g) ground chicken
- ➢ ¼ cup finely chopped ham
- ➢ ⅓ cup grated Havarti cheese
- ➢ Olive oil for misting

Instructions

1. Preheat the air fryer to 350°F (177°C). 2. In a medium bowl, combine the bread crumbs, milk, egg, thyme, salt, and pepper. Add the chicken and mix gently but thoroughly with clean hands. 3. Form the chicken into eight thin patties and place on waxed paper. 4. Top four of the patties with the ham and cheese. Top with remaining four patties and gently press the edges together to seal, so the ham and cheese mixture is in the middle of the burger. 5. Place the burgers in the basket and mist with olive oil. Bake for 13 to 16 minutes or until the chicken is thoroughly cooked to 165°F (74°C) as measured with a meat thermometer. Serve immediately.

Buffalo Chicken Wings

Preparation time: 10 minutes | Cook time: 20 to 25 minutes | Serves 4

- ➤ 2 tablespoons baking powder
- ➤ 1 teaspoon smoked paprika
- ➤ Sea salt and freshly ground black pepper, to taste
- ➤ 2 pounds (907 g) chicken wings or chicken drumettes
- ➤ Avocado oil spray
- ➤ ⅓ cup avocado oil
- ➤ ½ cup Buffalo hot sauce, such as Frank's RedHot
- ➤ ¼ cup (4 tablespoons) unsalted butter
- ➤ 2 tablespoons apple cider vinegar
- ➤ 1 teaspoon minced garlic

Instructions

1. In a large bowl, stir together the baking powder, smoked paprika, and salt and pepper to taste. Add the chicken wings and toss to coat. 2. Set the air fryer to 400°F (204°C). Spray the wings with oil. 3. Place the wings in the basket in a single layer, working in batches, and air fry for 20 to 25 minutes. Check with an instant-read thermometer and remove when they reach 155°F (68°C). Let rest until they reach 165°F (74°C). 4. While the wings are cooking, whisk together the avocado oil, hot sauce, butter, vinegar, and garlic in a small saucepan over medium-low heat until warm. 5. When the wings are done cooking, toss them with the Buffalo sauce. Serve warm.

Taco Chicken

Preparation time: 10 minutes | Cook time: 23 minutes | Serves 4

- ➤ 2 large eggs
- ➤ 1 tablespoon water
- ➤ Fine sea salt and ground black pepper, to taste
- ➤ 1 cup pork dust
- ➤ 1 teaspoon ground cumin
- ➤ 1 teaspoon smoked paprika
- ➤ 4 (5 ounces / 142 g) boneless, skinless chicken breasts or thighs, pounded to ¼ inch thick

- ➤ 1 cup salsa
- ➤ 1 cup shredded Monterey Jack cheese (about 4 ounces / 113 g) (omit for dairy-free)
- ➤ Sprig of fresh cilantro, for garnish (optional)

Instructions

1. Spray the air fryer basket with avocado oil. Preheat the air fryer to 400°F (204°C). 2. Crack the eggs into a shallow baking dish, add the water and a pinch each of salt and pepper, and whisk to combine. In another shallow baking dish, stir together the pork dust, cumin, and paprika until well combined. 3. Season the chicken breasts well on both sides with salt and pepper. Dip 1 chicken breast in the eggs and let any excess drip off, then dredge both sides of the chicken breast in the pork dust mixture. Spray the breast with avocado oil and place it in the air fryer basket. Repeat with the remaining 3 chicken breasts. 4. Air fry the chicken in the air fryer for 20 minutes, or until the internal temperature reaches 165°F (74°C) and the breading is golden brown, flipping halfway through. 5. Dollop each chicken breast with ¼ cup of the salsa and top with ¼ cup of the cheese. Return the breasts to the air fryer and cook for 3 minutes, or until the cheese is melted. Garnish with cilantro before serving, if desired. 6. Store leftovers in an airtight container in the refrigerator for up to 4 days. Reheat in a preheated 400°F (204°C) air fryer for 5 minutes, or until warmed through.

Easy Cajun Chicken Drumsticks

Preparation time: 5 minutes | Cook time: 40 minutes | Serves 5

- ➤ 1 tablespoon olive oil
- ➤ 10 chicken drumsticks
- ➤ 1½ tablespoons Cajun seasoning
- ➤ Salt and ground black pepper, to taste

Instructions

1. Preheat the air fryer to 390°F (199°C). Grease the air fryer basket with olive oil. 2. On a clean work surface, rub the chicken drumsticks with Cajun seasoning, salt, and ground black pepper. 3. Arrange the seasoned chicken drumsticks in a single layer in

the air fryer. You need to work in batches to avoid overcrowding. 4. Air fry for 18 minutes or until lightly browned. Flip the drumsticks halfway through. 5. Remove the chicken drumsticks from the air fryer. Serve immediately.

Juicy Paprika Chicken Breast

Preparation time: 5 minutes | Cook time: 30 minutes | Serves 4

- ➤ Oil, for spraying
- ➤ 4 (6-ounce / 170-g) boneless, skinless chicken breasts
- ➤ 1 tablespoon olive oil
- ➤ 1 tablespoon paprika
- ➤ 1 tablespoon packed light brown sugar
- ➤ ½ teaspoon cayenne pepper
- ➤ ½ teaspoon onion powder
- ➤ ½ teaspoon granulated garlic

Instructions

1. Line the air fryer basket with parchment and spray lightly with oil. 2. Brush the chicken with the olive oil. 3. In a small bowl, mix together the paprika, brown sugar, cayenne pepper, onion powder, and garlic and sprinkle it over the chicken. 4. Place the chicken in the prepared basket. You may need to work in batches, depending on the size of your air fryer. 5. Air fry at 360°F (182°C) for 15 minutes, flip, and cook for another 15 minutes, or until the internal temperature reaches 165°F (74°C). Serve immediately.

Ranch Chicken Wings

Preparation time: 10 minutes | Cook time: 40 minutes | Serves 4

- ➤ 2 tablespoons water
- ➤ 2 tablespoons hot pepper sauce
- ➤ 2 tablespoons unsalted butter, melted
- ➤ 2 tablespoons apple cider vinegar
- ➤ 1 (1-ounce / 28-g) envelope ranch salad dressing mix
- ➤ 1 teaspoon paprika

4 pounds (Instructions

1.8 kg) chicken wings, tips removed
- ➤ Cooking oil spray

Instructions

1. In a large bowl, whisk the water, hot pepper sauce, melted butter, vinegar, salad dressing mix, and paprika until combined. 2. Add the wings and toss to coat. At this point, you can cover the bowl and marinate the wings in the refrigerator for 4 to 24 hours for best results. However, you can just let the wings stand for 30 minutes in the refrigerator. 3. Insert the crisper plate into the basket and the basket into the unit. Preheat the unit by selecting AIR FRY, setting the temperature to 400°F (204°C), and setting the time to 3 minutes. Select START/STOP to begin. 4. Once the unit is preheated, spray the crisper plate with cooking oil. Working in batches, put half the wings into the basket; it is okay to stack them. Refrigerate the remaining wings. 5. Select AIR FRY, set the temperature to 400°F (204°C), and set the time to 20 minutes. Select START/STOP to begin. 6. After 5 minutes, remove the basket and shake it. Reinsert the basket to resume cooking. Remove and shake the basket every 5 minutes, three more times, until the chicken is browned and glazed and a food thermometer inserted into the wings registers 165°F (74°C). 7. Repeat steps 4, 5, and 6 with the remaining wings. 8. When the cooking is complete, serve warm.

Herb-Buttermilk Chicken Breast

Preparation time: 5 minutes | Cook time: 40 minutes | Serves 2

- ➤ 1 large bone-in, skin-on chicken breast
- ➤ 1 cup buttermilk
- ➤ 1½ teaspoons dried parsley
- ➤ 1½ teaspoons dried chives
- ➤ ¾ teaspoon kosher salt
- ➤ ½ teaspoon dried dill
- ➤ ½ teaspoon onion powder
- ➤ ¼ teaspoon garlic powder
- ➤ ¼ teaspoon dried tarragon
- ➤ Cooking spray

Instructions

1. Place the chicken breast in a bowl and pour over the buttermilk, turning the chicken in it to make sure it's completely covered. Let the chicken stand at room temperature for at least 20 minutes or in the

refrigerator for up to 4 hours. 2. Meanwhile, in a bowl, stir together the parsley, chives, salt, dill, onion powder, garlic powder, and tarragon. 3. Preheat the air fryer to 300°F (149°C). 4. Remove the chicken from the buttermilk, letting the excess drip off, then place the chicken skin-side up directly in the air fryer. Sprinkle the seasoning mix all over the top of the chicken breast, then let stand until the herb mix soaks into the buttermilk, at least 5 minutes. 5. Spray the top of the chicken with cooking spray. Bake for 10 minutes, then increase the temperature to 350°F (177°C) and bake until an instant-read thermometer inserted into the thickest part of the breast reads 160°F (71°C) and the chicken is deep golden brown, 30 to 35 minutes. 6. Transfer the chicken breast to a cutting board, let rest for 10 minutes, then cut the meat off the bone and cut into thick slices for serving.

Chicken Pesto Pizzas

Preparation time: 10 minutes | Cook time: 12 minutes | Serves 4

- 1 pound (454 g) ground chicken thighs
- ¼ teaspoon salt
- ⅛ teaspoon ground black pepper
- ¼ cup basil pesto
- 1 cup shredded Mozzarella cheese
- 4 grape tomatoes, sliced

Instructions

1. Cut four squares of parchment paper to fit into your air fryer basket. 2. Place ground chicken in a large bowl and mix with salt and pepper. Divide mixture into four equal sections. 3. Wet your hands with water to prevent sticking, then press each section into a 6-inch circle onto a piece of ungreased parchment. Place each chicken crust into air fryer basket, working in batches if needed. 4. Adjust the temperature to 350°F (177°C) and air fry for 10 minutes, turning crusts halfway through cooking. 5. Spread 1 tablespoon pesto across the top of each crust, then sprinkle with ¼ cup Mozzarella and top with 1 sliced tomato. Continue cooking at 350°F (177°C) for 2 minutes. Cheese will be melted and brown when done. Serve warm.

Chicken Legs with Leeks

Preparation time: 30 minutes | Cook time: 18 minutes | Serves 6

- 2 leeks, sliced
- 2 large-sized tomatoes, chopped
- 3 cloves garlic, minced
- ½ teaspoon dried oregano
- 6 chicken legs, boneless and skinless
- ½ teaspoon smoked cayenne pepper
- 2 tablespoons olive oil
- A freshly ground nutmeg

Instructions

1. In a mixing dish, thoroughly combine all ingredients, minus the leeks. Place in the refrigerator and let it marinate overnight. 2. Lay the leeks onto the bottom of the air fryer basket. Top with the chicken legs. 3. Roast chicken legs at 375°F (191°C) for 18 minutes, turning halfway through. Serve with hoisin sauce.

Stuffed Turkey Roulade

Preparation time: 10 minutes | Cook time: 45 minutes | Serves 4

- 1 (2-pound / 907-g) boneless turkey breast, skin removed
- 1 teaspoon salt
- ½ teaspoon black pepper
- 4 ounces (113 g) goat cheese
- 1 tablespoon fresh thyme
- 1 tablespoon fresh sage
- 2 garlic cloves, minced
- 2 tablespoons olive oil
- Fresh chopped parsley, for garnish

Instructions

1. Preheat the air fryer to 380°F(193°C). 2. Using a sharp knife, butterfly the turkey breast, and season both sides with salt and pepper and set aside. 3. In a small bowl, mix together the goat cheese, thyme, sage, and garlic. 4. Spread the cheese mixture over the turkey breast, then roll it up tightly, tucking the ends underneath. 5. Place the turkey breast roulade onto a piece of aluminum foil, wrap it up, and place it into the air fryer. 6. Bake for 30 minutes. Remove the foil from the turkey breast and brush the top with

oil, then continue cooking for another 10 to 15 minutes, or until the outside has browned and the internal temperature reaches 165°F(74°C). 7. Remove and cut into 1-inch-wide slices and serve with a sprinkle of parsley on top.

Jerk Chicken Kebabs

Preparation time: 10 minutes | Cook time: 14 minutes | Serves 4

- ➤ 8 ounces (227 g) boneless, skinless chicken thighs, cut into 1-inch cubes
- ➤ 2 tablespoons jerk seasoning
- ➤ 2 tablespoons coconut oil
- ➤ ½ medium red bell pepper, seeded and cut into 1-inch pieces
- ➤ ¼ medium red onion, peeled and cut into 1-inch pieces
- ➤ ½ teaspoon salt

Instructions

1. Place chicken in a medium bowl and sprinkle with jerk seasoning and coconut oil. Toss to coat on all sides. 2. Using eight (6-inch) skewers, build skewers by alternating chicken, pepper, and onion pieces, about three repetitions per skewer. 3. Sprinkle salt over skewers and place into ungreased air fryer basket. Adjust the temperature to 370°F (188°C) and air fry for 14 minutes, turning skewers halfway through cooking. Chicken will be golden and have an internal temperature of at least 165°F (74°C) when done. Serve warm.

Apricot Chicken

Preparation time: 15 minutes | Cook time: 10 to 12 minutes | Serves 4

- ➤ ⅔ cup apricot preserves
- ➤ 2 tablespoons freshly squeezed lemon juice
- ➤ 1 teaspoon soy sauce
- ➤ ¼ teaspoon salt
- ➤ ¾ cup panko bread crumbs

- ➤ 2 whole boneless, skinless chicken breasts (1 pound / 454 g each), halved
- ➤ 1 to 2 tablespoons oil

Instructions

1. In a shallow bowl, stir together the apricot preserves, lemon juice, soy sauce, and salt. Place the bread crumbs in a second shallow bowl. 2. Roll the chicken in the preserves mixture and then the bread crumbs, coating thoroughly. 3. Preheat the air fryer to 350°F (177°C). Line the air fryer basket with parchment paper. 4. Place the coated chicken on the parchment and spritz with oil. 5. Cook for 5 minutes. Flip the chicken, spritz it with oil, and cook for 5 to 7 minutes more until the internal temperature reaches 165°F (74°C) and the chicken is no longer pink inside. Let sit for 5 minutes.

Chipotle Drumsticks

Preparation time: 5 minutes | Cook time: 25 minutes | Serves 4

- ➤ 1 tablespoon tomato paste
- ➤ ½ teaspoon chipotle powder
- ➤ ¼ teaspoon apple cider vinegar
- ➤ ¼ teaspoon garlic powder
- ➤ 8 chicken drumsticks
- ➤ ½ teaspoon salt
- ➤ ⅛ teaspoon ground black pepper

Instructions

1. In a small bowl, combine tomato paste, chipotle powder, vinegar, and garlic powder. 2. Sprinkle drumsticks with salt and pepper, then place into a large bowl and pour in tomato paste mixture. Toss or stir to evenly coat all drumsticks in mixture. 3. Place drumsticks into ungreased air fryer basket. Adjust the temperature to 400°F (204°C) and air fry for 25 minutes, turning drumsticks halfway through cooking. Drumsticks will be dark red with an internal temperature of at least 165°F (74°C) when done. Serve warm.

CHAPTER 5 Beef, Pork, and Lamb

Bacon, Cheese and Pear Stuffed Pork

Preparation time: 10 minutes | Cook time: 24 minutes | Serves 3

➢ 4 slices bacon, chopped
➢ 1 tablespoon butter
➢ ½ cup finely diced onion
➢ ⅓ cup chicken stock
➢ 1½ cups seasoned stuffing cubes
➢ 1 egg, beaten
➢ ½ teaspoon dried thyme
➢ ½ teaspoon salt
➢ ⅛ teaspoon black pepper
➢ 1 pear, finely diced
➢ ⅓ cup crumbled blue cheese
➢ 3 boneless center-cut pork chops (2-inch thick)
➢ Olive oil
➢ Salt and freshly ground black pepper, to taste

Instructions

1. Preheat the air fryer to 400°F (204°C). 2. Place the bacon into the air fryer basket and air fry for 6 minutes, stirring halfway through the cooking time. Remove the bacon and set it aside on a paper towel. Pour out the grease from the bottom of the air fryer. 3. Make the stuffing: Melt the butter in a medium saucepan over medium heat on the stovetop. Add the onion and sauté for a few minutes, until it starts to soften. Add the chicken stock and simmer for 1 minute. Remove the pan from the heat and add the stuffing cubes. Stir until the stock has been absorbed. Add the egg, dried thyme, salt and freshly ground black pepper, and stir until combined. Fold in the diced pear and crumbled blue cheese. 4. Place the pork chops on a cutting board. Using the palm of your hand to hold the chop flat and steady, slice into the side of the pork chop to make a pocket in the center of the chop. Leave about an inch of chop uncut and make sure you don't cut all the way through the pork chop. Brush both sides of the pork chops with olive oil and season with salt and freshly ground black pepper. Stuff each pork chop with a third of the stuffing, packing the stuffing tightly inside the pocket. 5. Preheat the air fryer to 360°F (182°C). 6. Spray or brush the sides of the air fryer basket with oil. Place the pork chops in the air fryer basket with the open stuffed edge of the pork chop facing the outside edges of the basket. 7. Air fry the pork chops for 18 minutes, turning the pork chops over halfway through the cooking time. When the chops are done, let them rest for 5 minutes and then transfer to a serving platter.

Filipino Crispy Pork Belly

Preparation time: 20 minutes | Cook time: 30 minutes | Serves 4

➢ 1 pound (454 g) pork belly
➢ 3 cups water
➢ 6 garlic cloves
➢ 2 tablespoons soy sauce
➢ 1 teaspoon kosher salt
➢ 1 teaspoon black pepper
➢ 2 bay leaves

Instructions

1. Cut the pork belly into three thick chunks so it will cook more evenly. 2. Place the pork, water, garlic, soy sauce, salt, pepper, and bay leaves in the inner pot of an Instant Pot or other electric pressure cooker. Seal and cook at high pressure for 15 minutes. Let the pressure release naturally for 10 minutes, then manually release the remaining pressure. (If you do not have a pressure cooker, place all the ingredients in a large saucepan. Cover and cook over low heat until a knife can be easily inserted into the skin side of pork belly, about 1 hour.) Using tongs, very carefully transfer the meat to a wire rack over a rimmed baking sheet to drain and dry for 10 minutes.

3. Cut each chunk of pork belly into two long slices. Arrange the slices in the air fryer basket. Set the air fryer to 400°F (204°C) for 15 minutes, or until the fat has crisped. 4. Serve immediately.

Fruited Ham

Preparation time: 15 minutes | Cook time: 8 to 10 minutes | Serves 4

- ➢ 1 cup orange marmalade
- ➢ ¼ cup packed light brown sugar
- ➢ ¼ teaspoon ground cloves
- ➢ ½ teaspoon dry mustard
- ➢ 1 to 2 tablespoons oil
- ➢ 1 pound (454 g) cooked ham, cut into 1-inch cubes
- ➢ ½ cup canned mandarin oranges, drained and chopped

Instructions

1. In a small bowl, stir together the orange marmalade, brown sugar, cloves, and dry mustard until blended. Set aside. 2. Preheat the air fryer to 320°F (160°C). Spritz a baking pan with oil. 3. Place the ham cubes in the prepared pan. Pour the marmalade sauce over the ham to glaze it. 4. Cook for 4 minutes. Stir and cook for 2 minutes more. 5. Add the mandarin oranges and cook for 2 to 4 minutes more until the sauce begins to thicken and the ham is tender.

Smothered Chops

Preparation time: 20 minutes | Cook time: 30 minutes | Serves 4

- ➢ 4 bone-in pork chops (8 ounces / 227 g each)
- ➢ 2 teaspoons salt, divided
- ➢ 1½ teaspoons freshly ground black pepper, divided
- ➢ 1 teaspoon garlic powder
- ➢ 1 cup tomato purée
- ➢ 1½ teaspoons Italian seasoning
- ➢ 1 tablespoon sugar
- ➢ 1 tablespoon cornstarch
- ➢ ½ cup chopped onion
- ➢ ½ cup chopped green bell pepper
- ➢ 1 to 2 tablespoons oil

Instructions

1. Evenly season the pork chops with 1 teaspoon salt, 1 teaspoon pepper, and the garlic powder. 2. In a medium bowl, stir together the tomato purée, Italian seasoning, sugar, remaining 1 teaspoon of salt, and remaining ½ teaspoon of pepper. 3. In a small bowl, whisk ¾ cup water and the cornstarch until blended. Stir this slurry into the tomato purée, with the onion and green bell pepper. Transfer to a baking pan. 4. Preheat the air fryer to 350°F (177°C). 5. Place the sauce in the fryer and cook for 10 minutes. Stir and cook for 10 minutes more. Remove the pan and keep warm. 6. Increase the air fryer temperature to 400°F (204°C). Line the air fryer basket with parchment paper. 7. Place the pork chops on the parchment and spritz with oil. 8. Cook for 5 minutes. Flip and spritz the chops with oil and cook for 5 minutes more, until the internal temperature reaches 145°F (63°C). Serve with the tomato mixture spooned on top.

Swedish Meatloaf

Preparation time: 10 minutes | Cook time: 35 minutes | Serves 8

- ➢ 1½ pounds (680 g) ground beef (85% lean)
- ➢ ¼ pound (113 g) ground pork
- ➢ 1 large egg (omit for egg-free)
- ➢ ½ cup minced onions
- ➢ ¼ cup tomato sauce
- ➢ 2 tablespoons dry mustard
- ➢ 2 cloves garlic, minced
- ➢ 2 teaspoons fine sea salt
- ➢ 1 teaspoon ground black pepper, plus more for garnish
- ➢ Sauce:
- ➢ ½ cup (1 stick) unsalted butter
- ➢ ½ cup shredded Swiss or mild Cheddar cheese (about 2 ounces / 57 g)
- ➢ 2 ounces (57 g) cream cheese (¼ cup), softened
- ➢ ⅓ cup beef broth
- ➢ ⅛ teaspoon ground nutmeg
- ➢ Halved cherry tomatoes, for serving (optional)

Instructions

1. Preheat the air fryer to 390ºF (199ºC). 2. In a large bowl, combine the ground beef, ground pork, egg, onions, tomato sauce, dry mustard, garlic, salt, and pepper. Using your hands, mix until well combined. 3. Place the meatloaf mixture in a loaf pan and place it in the air fryer. Bake for 35 minutes, or until cooked through and the internal temperature reaches 145ºF (63ºC). Check the meatloaf after 25 minutes; if it's getting too brown on the top, cover it loosely with foil to prevent burning. 4. While the meatloaf cooks, make the sauce: Heat the butter in a saucepan over medium-high heat until it sizzles and brown flecks appear, stirring constantly to keep the butter from burning. Turn the heat down to low and whisk in the Swiss cheese, cream cheese, broth, and nutmeg. Simmer for at least 10 minutes. The longer it simmers, the more the flavors open up. 5. When the meatloaf is done, transfer it to a serving tray and pour the sauce over it. Garnish with ground black pepper and serve with cherry tomatoes, if desired. Allow the meatloaf to rest for 10 minutes before slicing so it doesn't crumble apart. 6. Store leftovers in an airtight container in the fridge for 3 days or in the freezer for up to a month. Reheat in a preheated 350ºF (177ºC) air fryer for 4 minutes, or until heated through.

Spicy Tomato Beef Meatballs

Preparation time: 10 minutes | Cook time: 15 minutes | Serves 4

- ➢ 3 scallions, minced
- ➢ 1 garlic clove, minced
- ➢ 1 egg yolk
- ➢ ¼ cup saltine cracker crumbs
- ➢ Pinch salt
- ➢ Freshly ground black pepper, to taste
- ➢ 1 pound (454 g) 95% lean ground beef
- ➢ Olive oil spray
- ➢ 1¼ cups any tomato pasta sauce (from a 16-ounce / 454-g jar)
- ➢ 2 tablespoons Dijon mustard

Instructions

1. In a large bowl, combine the scallions, garlic, egg yolk, cracker crumbs, salt, and pepper and mix well. 2. Add the ground beef and gently but thoroughly mix with your hands until combined. Form the meat mixture into 1½-inch round meatballs. 3. Insert the crisper plate into the basket and the basket into the unit. Preheat the unit by selecting BAKE, setting the temperature to 400ºF (204ºC), and setting the time to 3 minutes. Select START/STOP to begin. 4. Once the unit is preheated, spray the crisper plate with olive oil. Working in batches, spray the meatballs with olive oil and place them into the basket in a single layer, without touching. 5. Select BAKE, set the temperature to 400ºF (204ºC), and set the time to 11 minutes. Select START/STOP to begin. 6. When the cooking is complete, a food thermometer inserted into the meatballs should register 165ºF (74ºC). Transfer the meatballs to a 6-inch metal bowl. 7. Repeat steps 4, 5, and 6 with the remaining meatballs. 8. Top the meatballs with the pasta sauce and Dijon mustard, and mix gently. Place the bowl into the basket. 9. Select BAKE, set the temperature to 400ºF (204ºC), and set the time to 4 minutes. Select START/STOP to begin. 10. When the cooking is complete, serve hot.

Cheesy Low-Carb Lasagna

Preparation time: 10 minutes | Cook time: 10 minutes | Serves 4

- ➢ Meat Layer:
- ➢ Extra-virgin olive oil
- ➢ 1 pound (454 g) 85% lean ground beef
- ➢ 1 cup prepared marinara sauce
- ➢ ¼ cup diced celery
- ➢ ¼ cup diced red onion
- ➢ ½ teaspoon minced garlic
- ➢ Kosher salt and black pepper, to taste
- ➢ Cheese Layer:
- ➢ 8 ounces (227 g) ricotta cheese
- ➢ 1 cup shredded Mozzarella cheese
- ➢ ½ cup grated Parmesan cheese
- ➢ 2 large eggs
- ➢ 1 teaspoon dried Italian seasoning, crushed
- ➢ ½ teaspoon each minced garlic, garlic

powder, and black pepper

Instructions

1. For the meat layer: Grease a cake pan with 1 teaspoon olive oil. 2. In a large bowl, combine the ground beef, marinara, celery, onion, garlic, salt, and pepper. Place the seasoned meat in the pan. 3. Place the pan in the air fryer basket. Set the air fryer to 375°F (191°C) for 10 minutes. 4. Meanwhile, for the cheese layer: In a medium bowl, combine the ricotta, half the Mozzarella, the Parmesan, lightly beaten eggs, Italian seasoning, minced garlic, garlic powder, and pepper. Stir until well blended. 5. At the end of the cooking time, spread the cheese mixture over the meat mixture. Sprinkle with the remaining ½ cup Mozzarella. Set the air fryer to 375°F (191°C) for 10 minutes, or until the cheese is browned and bubbling. 6. At the end of the cooking time, use a meat thermometer to ensure the meat has reached an internal temperature of 160°F (71°C). 7. Drain the fat and liquid from the pan. Let stand for 5 minutes before serving.

Kheema Burgers

Preparation time: 15 minutes | Cook time: 12 minutes | Serves 4

➢ Burgers:
➢ 1 pound (454 g) 85% lean ground beef or ground lamb
➢ 2 large eggs, lightly beaten
➢ 1 medium yellow onion, diced
➢ ¼ cup chopped fresh cilantro
➢ 1 tablespoon minced fresh ginger
➢ 3 cloves garlic, minced
➢ 2 teaspoons garam masala
➢ 1 teaspoon ground turmeric
➢ ½ teaspoon ground cinnamon
➢ ⅛ teaspoon ground cardamom
➢ 1 teaspoon kosher salt
➢ 1 teaspoon cayenne pepper
➢ Raita Sauce:
➢ 1 cup grated cucumber
➢ ½ cup sour cream
➢ ¼ teaspoon kosher salt
➢ ¼ teaspoon black pepper

➢ For Serving:
➢ 4 lettuce leaves, hamburger buns, or naan breads

Instructions

1. For the burgers: In a large bowl, combine the ground beef, eggs, onion, cilantro, ginger, garlic, garam masala, turmeric, cinnamon, cardamom, salt, and cayenne. Gently mix until ingredients are thoroughly combined. 2. Divide the meat into four portions and form into round patties. Make a slight depression in the middle of each patty with your thumb to prevent them from puffing up into a dome shape while cooking. 3. Place the patties in the air fryer basket. Set the air fryer to 350°F (177°C) for 12 minutes. Use a meat thermometer to ensure the burgers have reached an internal temperature of 160°F / 71°C (for medium). 4. Meanwhile, for the sauce: In a small bowl, combine the cucumber, sour cream, salt, and pepper. 5. To serve: Place the burgers on the lettuce, buns, or naan and top with the sauce.

Beef Egg Rolls

Preparation time: 15 minutes | Cook time: 12 minutes | Makes 8 egg rolls

➢ ½ chopped onion
➢ 2 garlic cloves, chopped
➢ ½ packet taco seasoning
➢ Salt and ground black pepper, to taste
➢ 1 pound (454 g) lean ground beef
➢ ½ can cilantro lime rotel
➢ 16 egg roll wrappers
➢ 1 cup shredded Mexican cheese
➢ 1 tablespoon olive oil
➢ 1 teaspoon cilantro

Instructions

1. Preheat the air fryer to 400°F (205°C). 2. Add onions and garlic to a skillet, cooking until fragrant. Then add taco seasoning, pepper, salt, and beef, cooking until beef is broke up into tiny pieces and cooked thoroughly. 3. Add rotel and stir well. 4. Lay out egg wrappers and brush with a touch of water to soften a bit. 5. Load wrappers with beef filling and add cheese to each. 6. Fold diagonally to close and

use water to secure edges. 7. Brush filled egg wrappers with olive oil and add to the air fryer. 8. Air fry 8 minutes, flip, and air fry for another 4 minutes. 9. Serve sprinkled with cilantro.

Lamb Burger with Feta and Olives

Preparation time: 10 minutes | Cook time: 20 minutes | Serves 3 to 4

- ➤ 2 teaspoons olive oil
- ➤ ⅓ onion, finely chopped
- ➤ 1 clove garlic, minced
- ➤ 1 pound (454 g) ground lamb
- ➤ 2 tablespoons fresh parsley, finely chopped
- ➤ 1½ teaspoons fresh oregano, finely chopped
- ➤ ½ cup black olives, finely chopped
- ➤ ⅓ cup crumbled feta cheese
- ➤ ½ teaspoon salt
- ➤ Freshly ground black pepper, to taste
- ➤ 4 thick pita breads

Instructions

1. Preheat a medium skillet over medium-high heat on the stovetop. Add the olive oil and cook the onion until tender, but not browned, about 4 to 5 minutes. Add the garlic and cook for another minute. Transfer the onion and garlic to a mixing bowl and add the ground lamb, parsley, oregano, olives, feta cheese, salt and pepper. Gently mix the ingredients together. 2. Divide the mixture into 3 or 4 equal portions and then form the hamburgers, being careful not to over-handle the meat. One good way to do this is to throw the meat back and forth between your hands like a baseball, packing the meat each time you catch it. Flatten the balls into patties, making an indentation in the center of each patty. Flatten the sides of the patties as well to make it easier to fit them into the air fryer basket. 3. Preheat the air fryer to 370°F (188°C). 4. If you don't have room for all four burgers, air fry two or three burgers at a time for 8 minutes at 370°F (188°C). Flip the burgers over and air fry for another 8 minutes. If you cooked your burgers in batches, return the first batch of burgers to the air fryer for the last two minutes of cooking to re-heat. This should give you a medium-well burger. If you'd prefer a medium-rare burger, shorten the cooking time to about 13 minutes. Remove the burgers to a resting plate and let the burgers rest for a few minutes before dressing and serving. 5. While the burgers are resting, toast the pita breads in the air fryer for 2 minutes. Tuck the burgers into the toasted pita breads, or wrap the pitas around the burgers and serve with a tzatziki sauce or some mayonnaise.

Savory Sausage Cobbler

Preparation time: 15 minutes | Cook time: 34 minutes | Serves 4

- ➤ Filling:
- ➤ 1 pound (454 g) ground Italian sausage
- ➤ 1 cup sliced mushrooms
- ➤ 1 teaspoon fine sea salt
- ➤ 2 cups marinara sauce
- ➤ Biscuits:
- ➤ 3 large egg whites
- ➤ ¾ cup blanched almond flour
- ➤ 1 teaspoon baking powder
- ➤ ¼ teaspoon fine sea salt
- ➤ 2½ tablespoons very cold unsalted butter, cut into ¼-inch pieces
- ➤ Fresh basil leaves, for garnish

Instructions

1. Preheat the air fryer to 400°F (204°C). 2. Place the sausage in a pie pan (or a pan that fits into your air fryer). Use your hands to break up the sausage and spread it evenly on the bottom of the pan. Place the pan in the air fryer and air fry for 5 minutes. 3. Remove the pan from the air fryer and use a fork or metal spatula to crumble the sausage more. Season the mushrooms with the salt and add them to the pie pan. Stir to combine the mushrooms and sausage, then return the pan to the air fryer and air fry for 4 minutes, or until the mushrooms are soft and the sausage is cooked through. 4. Remove the pan from the air fryer. Add the marinara sauce and stir well. Set aside. 5. Make the biscuits: Place the egg whites in a large mixing bowl or the bowl of a stand mixer. Using a hand mixer or stand mixer, whip the egg

whites until stiff peaks form. 6. In a medium-sized bowl, whisk together the almond flour, baking powder, and salt, then cut in the butter. Gently fold the flour mixture into the egg whites with a rubber spatula. 7. Using a large spoon or ice cream scoop, spoon one-quarter of the dough on top of the sausage mixture, making sure the butter stays in separate clumps. Repeat with the remaining dough, spacing the biscuits about 1 inch apart. 8. Place the pan in the air fryer and cook for 5 minutes, then lower the heat to 325°F (163°C) and bake for another 15 to 20 minutes, until the biscuits are golden brown. Serve garnished with fresh basil leaves. 9. Store leftovers in an airtight container in the refrigerator for up to 3 days. Reheat in a preheated 350°F (177°C) air fryer for 5 minutes, or until warmed through.

Simple Ground Beef with Zucchini

Preparation time: 5 minutes | Cook time: 12 minutes | Serves 4

- 1½ pounds (680 g) ground beef
- 1 pound (454 g) chopped zucchini
- 2 tablespoons extra-virgin olive oil
- 1 teaspoon dried oregano
- 1 teaspoon dried basil
- 1 teaspoon dried rosemary
- 2 tablespoons fresh chives, chopped

Instructions

1. Preheat the air fryer to 400°F (204°C). 2. In a large bowl, combine all the ingredients, except for the chives, until well blended. 3. Place the beef and zucchini mixture in the baking pan. Air fry for 12 minutes, or until the beef is browned and the zucchini is tender. 4. Divide the beef and zucchini mixture among four serving dishes. Top with fresh chives and serve hot.

Pork and Pinto Bean Gorditas

Preparation time: 20 minutes | Cook time: 21 minutes | Serves 4

- 1 pound (454 g) lean ground pork
- 2 tablespoons chili powder
- 2 tablespoons ground cumin
- 1 teaspoon dried oregano
- 2 teaspoons paprika
- 1 teaspoon garlic powder
- ½ cup water
- 1 (15 ounces / 425 g) can pinto beans, drained and rinsed
- ½ cup taco sauce
- Salt and freshly ground black pepper, to taste
- 2 cups grated Cheddar cheese
- 5 (12-inch) flour tortillas
- 4 (8-inch) crispy corn tortilla shells
- 4 cups shredded lettuce
- 1 tomato, diced
- ⅓ cup sliced black olives
- Sour cream, for serving
- Tomato salsa, for serving
- Cooking spray

Instructions

1. Preheat the air fryer to 400°F (204°C). Spritz the air fryer basket with cooking spray. 2. Put the ground pork in the air fryer basket and air fry at 400°F (204°C) for 10 minutes, stirring a few times to gently break up the meat. Combine the chili powder, cumin, oregano, paprika, garlic powder and water in a small bowl. Stir the spice mixture into the browned pork. Stir in the beans and taco sauce and air fry for an additional minute. Transfer the pork mixture to a bowl. Season with salt and freshly ground black pepper. 3. Sprinkle ½ cup of the grated cheese in the center of the flour tortillas, leaving a 2-inch border around the edge free of cheese and filling. Divide the pork mixture among the four tortillas, placing it on top of the cheese. Put a crunchy corn tortilla on top of the pork and top with shredded lettuce, diced tomatoes, and black olives. Cut the remaining flour tortilla into 4 quarters. These quarters of tortilla will serve as the bottom of the gordita. Put one quarter tortilla on top of each gordita and fold the edges of the bottom flour tortilla up over the sides, enclosing the filling. While holding the seams down, brush the bottom of the gordita with olive oil and place the

seam side down on the countertop while you finish the remaining three gorditas. 4. Adjust the temperature to 380°F (193°C). 5. Air fry one gordita at a time. Transfer the gordita carefully to the air fryer basket, seam side down. Brush or spray the top tortilla with oil and air fry for 5 minutes. Carefully turn the gordita over and air fry for an additional 4 to 5 minutes until both sides are browned. When finished air frying all four gorditas, layer them back into the air fryer for an additional minute to make sure they are all warm before serving with sour cream and salsa.

Crescent Dogs

Preparation time: 15 minutes | Cook time: 8 minutes | Makes 24 crescent dogs

- ➤ Oil, for spraying
- ➤ 1 (8-ounce / 227-g) can refrigerated crescent rolls
- ➤ 8 slices Cheddar cheese, cut into thirds
- ➤ 24 cocktail sausages or 8 (6-inch) hot dogs, cut into thirds
- ➤ 2 tablespoons unsalted butter, melted
- ➤ 1 tablespoon sea salt flakes

Instructions

1. Line the air fryer basket with parchment and spray lightly with oil. 2. Separate the dough into 8 triangles. Cut each triangle into 3 narrow triangles so you have 24 total triangles. 3. Top each triangle with 1 piece of cheese and 1 cocktail sausage. 4. Roll up each piece of dough, starting at the wide end and rolling toward the point. 5. Place the rolls in the prepared basket in a single layer. You may need to cook in batches, depending on the size of your air fryer. 6. Air fry at 325°F (163°C) for 3 to 4 minutes, flip, and cook for another 3 to 4 minutes, or until golden brown. 7. Brush with the melted butter and sprinkle with the sea salt flakes before serving.

Chicken-Fried Steak

Preparation time: 20 minutes | Cook time: 14 minutes | Serves 2

- ➤ Steak:
- ➤ Oil, for spraying

- ➤ ¾ cup all-purpose flour
- ➤ 1 teaspoon salt
- ➤ 1 teaspoon freshly ground black pepper
- ➤ ½ teaspoon paprika
- ➤ ½ teaspoon onion powder
- ➤ 1 teaspoon granulated garlic
- ➤ ¾ cup buttermilk
- ➤ ½ teaspoon hot sauce
- ➤ 2 (5-ounce / 142-g) cube steaks
- ➤ Gravy:
- ➤ 2 tablespoons unsalted butter
- ➤ 2 tablespoons all-purpose flour
- ➤ 1 cup milk
- ➤ ½ teaspoon salt
- ➤ ½ teaspoon freshly ground black pepper

Make the Steak Instructions

1. Line the air fryer basket with parchment and spray lightly with oil. 2. In a medium bowl, mix together the flour, salt, black pepper, paprika, onion powder, and garlic. 3. In another bowl, whisk together the buttermilk and hot sauce. 4. Dredge the steaks in the flour mixture, dip in the buttermilk mixture, and dredge again in the flour until completely coated. Shake off any excess flour. 5. Place the steaks in the prepared basket and spray liberally with oil. 6. Air fry at 400°F (204°C) for 7 minutes, flip, spray with oil, and cook for another 6 to 7 minutes, or until crispy and browned. Make the Gravy 7. In a small saucepan, whisk together the butter and flour over medium heat until the butter is melted. Slowly add the milk, salt, and black pepper, increase the heat to medium-high, and continue to cook, stirring constantly, until the mixture thickens. Remove from the heat. 8. Transfer the steaks to plates and pour the gravy over the top. Serve immediately.

Easy Lamb Chops with Asparagus

Preparation time: 10 minutes | Cook time: 15 minutes | Serves 4

- ➤ 4 asparagus spears, trimmed
- ➤ 2 tablespoons olive oil, divided
- ➤ 1 pound (454 g) lamb chops
- ➤ 1 garlic clove, minced
- ➤ 2 teaspoons chopped fresh thyme, for

serving

➤ Salt and ground black pepper, to taste

Instructions

1. Preheat the air fryer to 400ºF (204ºC). Spritz the air fryer basket with cooking spray. 2. On a large plate, brush the asparagus with 1 tablespoon olive oil, then sprinkle with salt. Set aside. 3. On a separate plate, brush the lamb chops with remaining olive oil and sprinkle with salt and ground black pepper. 4. Arrange the lamb chops in the preheated air fryer. Air fry for 10 minutes. 5. Flip the lamb chops and add the asparagus and garlic. Air fry for 5 more minutes or until the lamb is well browned and the asparagus is tender. 6. Serve them on a plate with thyme on top.

Kale and Beef Omelet

Preparation time: 15 minutes | Cook time: 16 minutes | Serves 4

➤ ½ pound (227 g) leftover beef, coarsely chopped

➤ 2 garlic cloves, pressed

➤ 1 cup kale, torn into pieces and wilted

➤ 1 tomato, chopped

➤ ¼ teaspoon sugar

➤ 4 eggs, beaten

➤ 4 tablespoons heavy cream

➤ ½ teaspoon turmeric powder

➤ Salt and ground black pepper, to taste

➤ ⅛ teaspoon ground allspice

➤ Cooking spray

Instructions

1. Preheat the air fryer to 360ºF (182ºC). Spritz four ramekins with cooking spray. 2. Put equal amounts of each of the ingredients into each ramekin and mix well. 3. Air fry for 16 minutes. Serve immediately.

Mongolian-Style Beef

Preparation time: 10 minutes | Cook time: 10 minutes | Serves 4

➤ Oil, for spraying

➤ ¼ cup cornstarch

➤ 1 pound (454 g) flank steak, thinly sliced

➤ ¾ cup packed light brown sugar

➤ ½ cup soy sauce

➤ 2 teaspoons toasted sesame oil

➤ 1 tablespoon minced garlic

➤ ½ teaspoon ground ginger

➤ ½ cup water

➤ Cooked white rice or ramen noodles, for serving

Instructions

1. Line the air fryer basket with parchment and spray lightly with oil. 2. Place the cornstarch in a bowl and dredge the steak until evenly coated. Shake off any excess cornstarch. 3. Place the steak in the prepared basket and spray lightly with oil. 4. Roast at 390ºF (199ºC) for 5 minutes, flip, and cook for another 5 minutes. 5. In a small saucepan, combine the brown sugar, soy sauce, sesame oil, garlic, ginger, and water and bring to a boil over medium-high heat, stirring frequently. Remove from the heat. 6. Transfer the meat to the sauce and toss until evenly coated. Let sit for about 5 minutes so the steak absorbs the flavors. Serve with white rice or ramen noodles.

Pork Schnitzel with Dill Sauce

Preparation time: 5 minutes | Cook time: 24 minutes | Serves 4 to 6

➤ 6 boneless, center cut pork chops (about 1½ pounds / 680 g)

➤ ½ cup flour

➤ 1½ teaspoons salt

➤ Freshly ground black pepper, to taste

➤ 2 eggs

➤ ½ cup milk

➤ 1½ cups toasted fine bread crumbs

➤ 1 teaspoon paprika

➤ 3 tablespoons butter, melted

➤ 2 tablespoons vegetable or olive oil

➤ lemon wedges

➤ Dill Sauce:

➤ 1 cup chicken stock

➤ 1½ tablespoons cornstarch

➤ ⅓ cup sour cream

➤ 1½ tablespoons chopped fresh dill

➤ Salt and pepper, to taste

Instructions

1. Trim the excess fat from the pork chops and pound

each chop with a meat mallet between two pieces of plastic wrap until they are ½-inch thick. 2. Set up a dredging station. Combine the flour, salt, and black pepper in a shallow dish. Whisk the eggs and milk together in a second shallow dish. Finally, combine the bread crumbs and paprika in a third shallow dish. 3. Dip each flattened pork chop in the flour. Shake off the excess flour and dip each chop into the egg mixture. Finally dip them into the bread crumbs and press the bread crumbs onto the meat firmly. Place each finished chop on a baking sheet until they are all coated. 4. Preheat the air fryer to 400°F (204°C). 5. Combine the melted butter and the oil in a small bowl and lightly brush both sides of the coated pork chops. Do not brush the chops too heavily or the breading will not be as crispy. 6. Air fry one schnitzel at a time for 4 minutes, turning it over halfway through the cooking time. Hold the cooked schnitzels warm on a baking pan in a 170°F (77°C) oven while you finish air frying the rest. 7. While the schnitzels are cooking, whisk the chicken stock and cornstarch together in a small saucepan over medium-high heat on the stovetop. Bring the mixture to a boil and simmer for 2 minutes. Remove the saucepan from heat and whisk in the sour cream. Add the chopped fresh dill and season with salt and pepper. 8. Transfer the pork schnitzel to a platter and serve with dill sauce and lemon wedges.

Parmesan Herb Filet Mignon

Preparation time: 20 minutes | Cook time: 13 minutes | Serves 4

- ➢ 1 pound (454 g) filet mignon
- ➢ Sea salt and ground black pepper, to taste
- ➢ ½ teaspoon cayenne pepper
- ➢ 1 teaspoon dried basil
- ➢ 1 teaspoon dried rosemary
- ➢ 1 teaspoon dried thyme
- ➢ 1 tablespoon sesame oil
- ➢ 1 small-sized egg, well-whisked
- ➢ ½ cup Parmesan cheese, grated

Instructions

1. Season the filet mignon with salt, black pepper, cayenne pepper, basil, rosemary, and thyme. Brush with sesame oil. 2. Put the egg in a shallow plate. Now, place the Parmesan cheese in another plate. 3. Coat the filet mignon with the egg; then lay it into the Parmesan cheese. Set the air fryer to 360°F (182°C). 4. Cook for 10 to 13 minutes or until golden. Serve with mixed salad leaves and enjoy!

Spinach and Provolone Steak Rolls

Preparation time: 10 minutes | Cook time: 12 minutes | Makes 8 rolls

- ➢ 1 (1 pound / 454 g) flank steak, butterflied
- ➢ 8 (1 ounce / 28 g, ¼-inch-thick) deli slices provolone cheese
- ➢ 1 cup fresh spinach leaves
- ➢ ½ teaspoon salt
- ➢ ¼ teaspoon ground black pepper

Instructions

1. Place steak on a large plate. Place provolone slices to cover steak, leaving 1-inch at the edges. Lay spinach leaves over cheese. Gently roll steak and tie with kitchen twine or secure with toothpicks. Carefully slice into eight pieces. Sprinkle each with salt and pepper. 2. Place rolls into ungreased air fryer basket, cut side up. Adjust the temperature to 400°F (204°C) and air fry for 12 minutes. Steak rolls will be browned and cheese will be melted when done and have an internal temperature of at least 150°F (66°C) for medium steak and 180°F (82°C) for well-done steak. Serve warm.

Rosemary Ribeye Steaks

Preparation time: 10 minutes | Cook time: 15 minutes | Serves 2

- ➢ ¼ cup butter
- ➢ 1 clove garlic, minced
- ➢ Salt and ground black pepper, to taste
- ➢ 1½ tablespoons balsamic vinegar
- ➢ ¼ cup rosemary, chopped
- ➢ 2 ribeye steaks

Instructions

1. Melt the butter in a skillet over medium heat. Add

the garlic and fry until fragrant. 2. Remove the skillet from the heat and add the salt, pepper, and vinegar. Allow it to cool. 3. Add the rosemary, then pour the mixture into a Ziploc bag. 4. Put the ribeye steaks in the bag and shake well, coating the meat well. Refrigerate for an hour, then allow to sit for a further twenty minutes. 5. Preheat the air fryer to 400°F (204°C). 6. Air fry the ribeye steaks for 15 minutes. 7. Take care when removing the steaks from the air fryer and plate up. 8. Serve immediately.

Garlic-Marinated Flank Steak

Preparation time: 30 minutes | Cook time: 8 to 10 minutes | Serves 6

- ½ cup avocado oil
- ¼ cup coconut aminos
- 1 shallot, minced
- 1 tablespoon minced garlic
- 2 tablespoons chopped fresh oregano, or 2 teaspoons dried
- 1½ teaspoons sea salt
- 1 teaspoon freshly ground black pepper
- ¼ teaspoon red pepper flakes
- 2 pounds (907 g) flank steak

Instructions

1. In a blender, combine the avocado oil, coconut aminos, shallot, garlic, oregano, salt, black pepper, and red pepper flakes. Process until smooth. 2. Place the steak in a zip-top plastic bag or shallow dish with the marinade. Seal the bag or cover the dish and marinate in the refrigerator for at least 2 hours or overnight. 3. Remove the steak from the bag and discard the marinade. 4. Set the air fryer to 400°F (204°C). Place the steak in the air fryer basket (if needed, cut into sections and work in batches). Air fry for 4 to 6 minutes, flip the steak, and cook for another 4 minutes or until the internal temperature reaches 120°F (49°C) in the thickest part for medium-rare (or as desired).

Mustard Herb Pork Tenderloin

Preparation time: 5 minutes | Cook time: 20 minutes | Serves 6

- ¼ cup mayonnaise
- 2 tablespoons Dijon mustard

- ½ teaspoon dried thyme
- ¼ teaspoon dried rosemary
- 1 (1 pound / 454 g) pork tenderloin
- ½ teaspoon salt
- ¼ teaspoon ground black pepper

Instructions

1. In a small bowl, mix mayonnaise, mustard, thyme, and rosemary. Brush tenderloin with mixture on all sides, then sprinkle with salt and pepper on all sides. 2. Place tenderloin into ungreased air fryer basket. Adjust the temperature to 400°F (204°C) and air fry for 20 minutes, turning tenderloin halfway through cooking. Tenderloin will be golden and have an internal temperature of at least 145°F (63°C) when done. Serve warm.

Dijon Porterhouse Steak

Preparation time: 20 minutes | Cook time: 14 minutes | Serves 2

- 1 pound (454 g) porterhouse steak, cut meat from bones in 2 pieces
- ½ teaspoon ground black pepper
- 1 teaspoon cayenne pepper
- ½ teaspoon salt
- 1 teaspoon garlic powder
- ½ teaspoon dried thyme
- ½ teaspoon dried marjoram
- 1 teaspoon Dijon mustard
- 1 tablespoon butter, melted

Instructions

1. Sprinkle the porterhouse steak with all the seasonings. 2. Spread the mustard and butter evenly over the meat. 3. Cook in the preheated air fryer at 390°F (199°C) for 12 to 14 minutes. 4. Taste for doneness with a meat thermometer and serve immediately.

BBQ Pork Steaks

Preparation time: 5 minutes | Cook time: 15 minutes | Serves 4

- 4 pork steaks
- 1 tablespoon Cajun seasoning
- 2 tablespoons BBQ sauce
- 1 tablespoon vinegar
- 1 teaspoon soy sauce

- ➤ ½ cup brown sugar
- ➤ ½ cup ketchup

Instructions

1. Preheat the air fryer to 290°F (143°C). 2. Sprinkle pork steaks with Cajun seasoning. 3. Combine remaining ingredients and brush onto steaks. 4. Add coated steaks to air fryer. Air fry 15 minutes until just browned. 5. Serve immediately.

Bulgogi Burgers

Preparation time: 30 minutes | Cook time: 10 minutes | Serves 4

- ➤ Burgers:
- ➤ 1 pound (454 g) 85% lean ground beef
- ➤ ¼ cup chopped scallions
- ➤ 2 tablespoons gochujang (Korean red chile paste)
- ➤ 1 tablespoon dark soy sauce
- ➤ 2 teaspoons minced garlic
- ➤ 2 teaspoons minced fresh ginger
- ➤ 2 teaspoons sugar
- ➤ 1 tablespoon toasted sesame oil
- ➤ ½ teaspoon kosher salt
- ➤ Gochujang Mayonnaise:
- ➤ ¼ cup mayonnaise
- ➤ ¼ cup chopped scallions
- ➤ 1 tablespoon gochujang (Korean red chile paste)
- ➤ 1 tablespoon toasted sesame oil
- ➤ 2 teaspoons sesame seeds
- ➤ 4 hamburger buns

Instructions

1. For the burgers: In a large bowl, mix the ground beef, scallions, gochujang, soy sauce, garlic, ginger, sugar, sesame oil, and salt. Marinate at room temperature for 30 minutes, or cover and refrigerate for up to 24 hours. 2. Divide the meat into four portions and form them into round patties. Make a slight depression in the middle of each patty with your thumb to prevent them from puffing up into a dome shape while cooking. 3. Place the patties in a single layer in the air fryer basket. Set the air fryer to 350°F (177°C) for 10 minutes. 4. Meanwhile, for the gochujang mayonnaise: Stir together the mayonnaise,

scallions, gochujang, sesame oil, and sesame seeds. 5. At the end of the cooking time, use a meat thermometer to ensure the burgers have reached an internal temperature of 160°F / 71°C (medium). 6. To serve, place the burgers on the buns and top with the mayonnaise.

Tenderloin with Crispy Shallots

Preparation time: 30 minutes | Cook time: 18 to 20 minutes | Serves 6

- ➤ 1½ pounds (680 g) beef tenderloin steaks
- ➤ Sea salt and freshly ground black pepper, to taste
- ➤ 4 medium shallots
- ➤ 1 teaspoon olive oil or avocado oil

Instructions

1. Season both sides of the steaks with salt and pepper, and let them sit at room temperature for 45 minutes. 2. Set the air fryer to 400°F (204°C) and let it preheat for 5 minutes. 3. Working in batches if necessary, place the steaks in the air fryer basket in a single layer and air fry for 5 minutes. Flip and cook for 5 minutes longer, until an instant-read thermometer inserted in the center of the steaks registers 120°F (49°C) for medium-rare (or as desired). Remove the steaks and tent with aluminum foil to rest. 4. Set the air fryer to 300°F (149°C). In a medium bowl, toss the shallots with the oil. Place the shallots in the basket and air fry for 5 minutes, then give them a toss and cook for 3 to 5 minutes more, until crispy and golden brown. 5. Place the steaks on serving plates and arrange the shallots on top.

Ham with Sweet Potatoes

Preparation time: 20 minutes | Cook time: 15 to 17 minutes | Serves 4

- ➤ 1 cup freshly squeezed orange juice
- ➤ ½ cup packed light brown sugar
- ➤ 1 tablespoon Dijon mustard
- ➤ ½ teaspoon salt
- ➤ ½ teaspoon freshly ground black pepper
- ➤ 3 sweet potatoes, cut into small wedges
- ➤ 2 ham steaks (8 ounces / 227 g each), halved

➢ 1 to 2 tablespoons oil

Instructions

1. In a large bowl, whisk the orange juice, brown sugar, Dijon, salt, and pepper until blended. Toss the sweet potato wedges with the brown sugar mixture. 2. Preheat the air fryer to 400°F (204°C). Line the air fryer basket with parchment paper and spritz with oil. 3. Place the sweet potato wedges on the parchment. 4. Cook for 10 minutes. 5. Place ham steaks on top of the sweet potatoes and brush everything with more of the orange juice mixture. 6. Cook for 3 minutes. Flip the ham and cook or 2 to 4 minutes more until the sweet potatoes are soft and the glaze has thickened. Cut the ham steaks in half to serve.

Deconstructed Chicago Dogs

Preparation time: 10 minutes | Cook time: 7 minutes | Serves 4

➢ 4 hot dogs
➢ 2 large dill pickles
➢ ¼ cup diced onions
➢ 1 tomato, cut into ½-inch dice
➢ 4 pickled sport peppers, diced
➢ For Garnish (Optional):
➢ Brown mustard
➢ Celery salt
➢ Poppy seeds

Instructions

1. Spray the air fryer basket with avocado oil. Preheat the air fryer to 400°F (204°C). 2. Place the hot dogs in the air fryer basket and air fry for 5 to 7 minutes, until hot and slightly crispy. 3. While the hot dogs cook, quarter one of the dill pickles lengthwise, so that you have 4 pickle spears. Finely dice the other pickle. 4. When the hot dogs are done, transfer them to a serving platter and arrange them in a row, alternating with the pickle spears. Top with the diced pickles, onions, tomato, and sport peppers. Drizzle brown mustard on top and garnish with celery salt and poppy seeds, if desired. 5. Best served fresh. Store leftover hot dogs in an airtight container in the refrigerator for up to 3 days. Reheat in a preheated 390°F (199°C) air fryer for 2 minutes, or until warmed through.

Kheema Meatloaf

Preparation time: 10 minutes | Cook time: 15 minutes | Serves 4

➢ 1 pound (454 g) 85% lean ground beef
➢ 2 large eggs, lightly beaten
➢ 1 cup diced yellow onion
➢ ¼ cup chopped fresh cilantro
➢ 1 tablespoon minced fresh ginger
➢ 1 tablespoon minced garlic
➢ 2 teaspoons garam masala
➢ 1 teaspoon kosher salt
➢ 1 teaspoon ground turmeric
➢ 1 teaspoon cayenne pepper
➢ ½ teaspoon ground cinnamon
➢ ⅛ teaspoon ground cardamom

Instructions

1. In a large bowl, gently mix the ground beef, eggs, onion, cilantro, ginger, garlic, garam masala, salt, turmeric, cayenne, cinnamon, and cardamom until thoroughly combined. 2. Place the seasoned meat in a baking pan. Place the pan in the air fryer basket. Set the air fryer to 350°F (177°C) for 15 minutes. Use a meat thermometer to ensure the meat loaf has reached an internal temperature of 160°F / 71°C (medium). 3. Drain the fat and liquid from the pan and let stand for 5 minutes before slicing. 4. Slice and serve hot.

CHAPTER 6 Fish and Seafood

Simple Buttery Cod

Preparation time: 5 minutes | Cook time: 8 minutes | Serves 2

- 2 (4-ounce / 113-g) cod fillets
- 2 tablespoons salted butter, melted
- 1 teaspoon Old Bay seasoning
- ½ medium lemon, sliced

Instructions

1. Place cod fillets into a round baking dish. Brush each fillet with butter and sprinkle with Old Bay seasoning. Lay two lemon slices on each fillet. Cover the dish with foil and place into the air fryer basket. 2. Adjust the temperature to 350°F (177°C) and bake for 8 minutes. 3. Flip halfway through the cooking time. When cooked, internal temperature should be at least 145°F (63°C). Serve warm.

Lemon-Pepper Trout

Preparation time: 5 minutes | Cook time: 15 minutes | Serves 4

- 4 trout fillets
- 2 tablespoons olive oil
- ½ teaspoon salt
- 1 teaspoon black pepper
- 2 garlic cloves, sliced
- 1 lemon, sliced, plus additional wedges for serving

Instructions

1. Preheat the air fryer to 380°F(193°C). 2. Brush each fillet with olive oil on both sides and season with salt and pepper. Place the fillets in an even layer in the air fryer basket. 3. Place the sliced garlic over the tops of the trout fillets, then top the garlic with lemon slices and roast for 12 to 15 minutes, or until it has reached an internal temperature of 145°F(63°C). 4. Serve with fresh lemon wedges.

Tuna Steak

Preparation time: 10 minutes | Cook time: 12 minutes | Serves 4

- 1 pound (454 g) tuna steaks, boneless and cubed
- 1 tablespoon mustard
- 1 tablespoon avocado oil
- 1 tablespoon apple cider vinegar

Instructions

1. Mix avocado oil with mustard and apple cider vinegar. 2. Then brush tuna steaks with mustard mixture and put in the air fryer basket. 3. Cook the fish at 360°F (182°C) for 6 minutes per side.

Parmesan Lobster Tails

Preparation time: 5 minutes | Cook time: 7 minutes | Serves 4

- 4 (4 ounces / 113 g) lobster tails
- 2 tablespoons salted butter, melted
- 1½ teaspoons Cajun seasoning, divided
- ¼ teaspoon salt
- ¼ teaspoon ground black pepper
- ¼ cup grated Parmesan cheese
- ½ ounce (14 g) plain pork rinds, finely crushed

Instructions

1. Cut lobster tails open carefully with a pair of scissors and gently pull meat away from shells, resting meat on top of shells. 2. Brush lobster meat with butter and sprinkle with 1 teaspoon Cajun seasoning, ¼ teaspoon per tail. 3. In a small bowl, mix remaining Cajun seasoning, salt, pepper, Parmesan, and pork rinds. Gently press ¼ mixture onto meat on each lobster tail. 4. Carefully place tails into ungreased air fryer basket. Adjust the temperature to 400°F (204°C) and air fry for 7 minutes. Lobster tails will be crispy and golden on top and have an internal temperature of at least 145°F (63°C) when done. Serve warm.

Salmon Patties

Preparation time: 5 minutes | Cook time: 8 minutes | Serves 4

- 12 ounces (340 g) pouched pink salmon
- 3 tablespoons mayonnaise
- ⅓ cup blanched finely ground almond flour
- ½ teaspoon Cajun seasoning
- 1 medium avocado, peeled, pitted, and sliced

Instructions

1. In a medium bowl, mix salmon, mayonnaise, flour, and Cajun seasoning. Form mixture into four patties. 2. Place patties into ungreased air fryer basket. Adjust the temperature to 400°F (204°C) and air fry for 8 minutes, turning patties halfway through cooking. Patties will be done when firm and golden brown. 3. Transfer patties to four medium plates and serve warm with avocado slices.

Tilapia with Pecans

Preparation time: 20 minutes | Cook time: 16 minutes | Serves 5

- 2 tablespoons ground flaxseeds
- 1 teaspoon paprika
- Sea salt and white pepper, to taste
- 1 teaspoon garlic paste
- 2 tablespoons extra-virgin olive oil
- ½ cup pecans, ground
- 5 tilapia fillets, sliced into halves

Instructions

1. Combine the ground flaxseeds, paprika, salt, white pepper, garlic paste, olive oil, and ground pecans in a Ziploc bag. Add the fish fillets and shake to coat well. 2. Spritz the air fryer basket with cooking spray. Cook in the preheated air fryer at 400°F (204°C) for 10 minutes; turn them over and cook for 6 minutes more. Work in batches. 3. Serve with lemon wedges, if desired. Enjoy!

Crab Cakes with Mango Mayo

Preparation time: 25 minutes | Cook time: 15 minutes | Serves 4

- Crab Cakes:
- ½ cup chopped red onion
- ½ cup fresh cilantro leaves
- 1 small serrano chile or jalapeño, seeded

and quartered
- ½ pound (227 g) lump crab meat
- 1 large egg
- 1 tablespoon mayonnaise
- 1 tablespoon whole-grain mustard
- 2 teaspoons minced fresh ginger
- ½ teaspoon ground cumin
- ½ teaspoon ground coriander
- ¼ teaspoon kosher salt
- 2 tablespoons fresh lemon juice
- 1½ cups panko bread crumbs
- Vegetable oil spray
- Mango Mayo:
- ½ cup diced fresh mango
- ½ cup mayonnaise
- ½ teaspoon grated lime zest
- 2 teaspoons fresh lime juice
- Pinch of cayenne pepper

Instructions

1. For the crab cakes: Combine the onion, cilantro, and serrano in a food processor. Pulse until minced. 2. In a large bowl, combine the minced vegetable mixture with the crab meat, egg, mayonnaise, mustard, ginger, cumin, coriander, and salt. Add the lemon juice and mix gently until thoroughly combined. Add 1 cup of the bread crumbs. Mix gently again until well blended. 3. Form into four evenly sized patties. Put the remaining ½ cup bread crumbs in a shallow bowl and press both sides of each patty into the bread crumbs. 4. Arrange the patties in the air fryer basket. Spray with vegetable oil spray. Set the air fryer to 375°F (191°C) for 15 minutes, turning and spraying other side of the patties with vegetable oil spray halfway through the cooking time, until the crab cakes are golden brown and crisp. 5. Meanwhile, for the mayonnaise: In a blender, combine the mango, mayonnaise, lime zest, lime juice, and cayenne. Blend until smooth. 6. Serve the crab cakes warm, with the mango mayo.

Blackened Salmon

Preparation time: 10 minutes | Cook time: 8 minutes | Serves 2

- 10 ounces (283 g) salmon fillet

- ½ teaspoon ground coriander
- 1 teaspoon ground cumin
- 1 teaspoon dried basil
- 1 tablespoon avocado oil

Instructions

1. In the shallow bowl, mix ground coriander, ground cumin, and dried basil. 2. Then coat the salmon fillet in the spices and sprinkle with avocado oil. 3. Put the fish in the air fryer basket and cook at 395°F (202°C) for 4 minutes per side.

Smoky Shrimp and Chorizo Tapas

Preparation time: 15 minutes | Cook time: 10 minutes | Serves 2 to 4

- 4 ounces (113 g) Spanish (cured) chorizo, halved horizontally and sliced crosswise
- ½ pound (227 g) raw medium shrimp, peeled and deveined
- 1 tablespoon extra-virgin olive oil
- 1 small shallot, halved and thinly sliced
- 1 garlic clove, minced
- 1 tablespoon finely chopped fresh oregano
- ½ teaspoon smoked Spanish paprika
- ¼ teaspoon kosher salt
- ¼ teaspoon black pepper
- 3 tablespoons fresh orange juice
- 1 tablespoon minced fresh parsley

Instructions

1. Place the chorizo in a baking pan. Set the pan in the air fryer basket. Set the air fryer to 375°F (191°C) for 5 minutes, or until the chorizo has started to brown and render its fat. 2. Meanwhile, in a large bowl, combine the shrimp, olive oil, shallot, garlic, oregano, paprika, salt, and pepper. Toss until the shrimp is well coated. 3. Transfer the shrimp to the pan with the chorizo. Stir to combine. Place the pan in the air fryer basket. Cook for 10 minutes, stirring halfway through the cooking time. 4. Transfer the shrimp and chorizo to a serving dish. Drizzle with the orange juice and toss to combine. Sprinkle with the parsley.

Sea Bass with Roasted Root Vegetables

Preparation time: 10 minutes | Cook time: 15 minutes | Serves 4

- 1 carrot, diced small
- 1 parsnip, diced small
- 1 rutabaga, diced small
- ¼ cup olive oil
- 1 teaspoon salt, divided
- 4 sea bass fillets
- ½ teaspoon onion powder
- 2 garlic cloves, minced
- 1 lemon, sliced, plus additional wedges for serving

Instructions

1. Preheat the air fryer to 380°F(193°C). 2. In a small bowl, toss the carrot, parsnip, and rutabaga with olive oil and 1 teaspoon salt. 3. Lightly season the sea bass with the remaining 1 teaspoon of salt and the onion powder, then place it into the air fryer basket in a single layer. 4. Spread the garlic over the top of each fillet, then cover with lemon slices. 5. Pour the prepared vegetables into the basket around and on top of the fish. Roast for 15 minutes. 6. Serve with additional lemon wedges if desired.

Oyster Po'Boy

Preparation time: 20 minutes | Cook time: 5 minutes | Serves 4

- ¾ cup all-purpose flour
- ¼ cup yellow cornmeal
- 1 tablespoon Cajun seasoning
- 1 teaspoon salt
- 2 large eggs, beaten
- 1 teaspoon hot sauce
- 1 pound (454 g) pre-shucked oysters
- 1 (12-inch) French baguette, quartered and sliced horizontally
- Tartar Sauce, as needed
- 2 cups shredded lettuce, divided
- 2 tomatoes, cut into slices
- Cooking spray

Instructions

1. In a shallow bowl, whisk the flour, cornmeal, Cajun seasoning, and salt until blended. In a second shallow bowl, whisk together the eggs and hot sauce. 2. One at a time, dip the oysters in the cornmeal mixture, the eggs, and again in the cornmeal, coating thoroughly. 3. Preheat the air fryer to 400°F (204°C). Line the air fryer basket with parchment paper. 4. Place the oysters on the parchment and spritz with oil. 5. Air fry for 2 minutes. Shake the basket, spritz the oysters with oil, and air fry for 3 minutes more until lightly browned and crispy. 6. Spread each sandwich half with Tartar Sauce. Assemble the po'boys by layering each sandwich with fried oysters, ½ cup shredded lettuce, and 2 tomato slices. 7. Serve immediately.

Pecan-Crusted Catfish

Preparation time: 5 minutes | Cook time: 12 minutes | Serves 4

- ½ cup pecan meal
- 1 teaspoon fine sea salt
- ¼ teaspoon ground black pepper
- 4 (4 ounces / 113 g) catfish fillets
- For Garnish (Optional):
- Fresh oregano
- Pecan halves

Instructions

1. Spray the air fryer basket with avocado oil. Preheat the air fryer to 375°F (191°C). 2. In a large bowl, mix the pecan meal, salt, and pepper. One at a time, dredge the catfish fillets in the mixture, coating them well. Use your hands to press the pecan meal into the fillets. Spray the fish with avocado oil and place them in the air fryer basket. 3. Air fry the coated catfish for 12 minutes, or until it flakes easily and is no longer translucent in the center, flipping halfway through. 4. Garnish with oregano sprigs and pecan halves, if desired. 5. Store leftovers in an airtight container in the fridge for up to 3 days. Reheat in a preheated 350°F (177°C) air fryer for 4 minutes, or until heated through.

Garlic Butter Shrimp Scampi

Preparation time: 5 minutes | Cook time: 8 minutes | Serves 4

- Sauce:
- ¼ cup unsalted butter
- 2 tablespoons fish stock or chicken broth
- 2 cloves garlic, minced
- 2 tablespoons chopped fresh basil leaves
- 1 tablespoon lemon juice
- 1 tablespoon chopped fresh parsley, plus more for garnish
- 1 teaspoon red pepper flakes
- Shrimp:
- 1 pound (454 g) large shrimp, peeled and deveined, tails removed
- Fresh basil sprigs, for garnish

Instructions

1. Preheat the air fryer to 350°F (177°C). 2. Put all the ingredients for the sauce in a baking pan and stir to incorporate. 3. Transfer the baking pan to the air fryer and air fry for 3 minutes, or until the sauce is heated through. 4. Once done, add the shrimp to the baking pan, flipping to coat in the sauce. 5. Return to the air fryer and cook for another 5 minutes, or until the shrimp are pink and opaque. Stir the shrimp twice during cooking. 6. Serve garnished with the parsley and basil sprigs.

Panko-Crusted Fish Sticks

Preparation time: 10 minutes | Cook time: 15 minutes | Serves 4

- Tartar Sauce:
- 2 cups mayonnaise
- 2 tablespoons dill pickle relish
- 1 tablespoon dried minced onions
- Fish Sticks:
- Oil, for spraying
- 1 pound (454 g) tilapia fillets
- ½ cup all-purpose flour
- 2 cups panko bread crumbs
- 2 tablespoons Creole seasoning
- 2 teaspoons granulated garlic
- 1 teaspoon onion powder
- ½ teaspoon salt
- ¼ teaspoon freshly ground black pepper
- 1 large egg

Make the Tartar Sauce Instructions

1. In a small bowl, whisk together the mayonnaise, pickle relish, and onions. Cover with plastic wrap and refrigerate until ready to serve. You can make this sauce ahead of time; the flavors will intensify as it chills. Make the Fish Sticks 2. Preheat the air fryer to 350°F (177°C). Line the air fryer basket with parchment and spray lightly with oil. 3. Cut the fillets into equal-size sticks and place them in a zip-top plastic bag. 4. Add the flour to the bag, seal, and shake well until evenly coated. 5. In a shallow bowl, mix together the bread crumbs, Creole seasoning, garlic, onion powder, salt, and black pepper. 6. In a small bowl, whisk the egg. 7. Dip the fish sticks in the egg, then dredge in the bread crumb mixture until completely coated. 8. Place the fish sticks in the prepared basket. You may need to work in batches, depending on the size of your air fryer. Do not overcrowd. Spray lightly with oil. 9. Cook for 12 to 15 minutes, or until browned and cooked through. Serve with the tartar sauce.

Marinated Swordfish Skewers

Preparation time: 30 minutes | Cook time: 6 to 8 minutes | Serves 4

➢ 1 pound (454 g) filleted swordfish
➢ ¼ cup avocado oil
➢ 2 tablespoons freshly squeezed lemon juice
➢ 1 tablespoon minced fresh parsley
➢ 2 teaspoons Dijon mustard
➢ Sea salt and freshly ground black pepper, to taste
➢ 3 ounces (85 g) cherry tomatoes

Instructions

1. Cut the fish into 1½-inch chunks, picking out any remaining bones. 2. In a large bowl, whisk together the oil, lemon juice, parsley, and Dijon mustard. Season to taste with salt and pepper. Add the fish and toss to coat the pieces. Cover and marinate the fish chunks in the refrigerator for 30 minutes. 3. Remove the fish from the marinade. Thread the fish and cherry tomatoes on 4 skewers, alternating as you go. 4. Set the air fryer to 400°F (204°C). Place the skewers in the air fryer basket and air fry for 3

minutes. Flip the skewers and cook for 3 to 5 minutes longer, until the fish is cooked through and an instant-read thermometer reads 140°F (60°C).

Shrimp Caesar Salad

Preparation time: 30 minutes | Cook time: 4 to 6 minutes | Serves 4

➢ 12 ounces (340 g) fresh large shrimp, peeled and deveined
➢ 1 tablespoon plus 1 teaspoon freshly squeezed lemon juice, divided
➢ 4 tablespoons olive oil or avocado oil, divided
➢ 2 garlic cloves, minced, divided
➢ ¼ teaspoon sea salt, plus additional to season the marinade
➢ ¼ teaspoon freshly ground black pepper, plus additional to season the marinade
➢ ⅓ cup sugar-free mayonnaise
➢ 2 tablespoons freshly grated Parmesan cheese
➢ 1 teaspoon Dijon mustard
➢ 1 tinned anchovy, mashed
➢ 12 ounces (340 g) romaine hearts, torn

Instructions

1. Place the shrimp in a large bowl. Add 1 tablespoon of lemon juice, 1 tablespoon of olive oil, and 1 minced garlic clove. Season with salt and pepper. Toss well and refrigerate for 15 minutes. 2. While the shrimp marinates, make the dressing: In a blender, combine the mayonnaise, Parmesan cheese, Dijon mustard, the remaining 1 teaspoon of lemon juice, the anchovy, the remaining minced garlic clove, ¼ teaspoon of salt, and ¼ teaspoon of pepper. Process until smooth. With the blender running, slowly stream in the remaining 3 tablespoons of oil. Transfer the mixture to a jar; seal and refrigerate until ready to serve. 3. Remove the shrimp from its marinade and place it in the air fryer basket in a single layer. Set the air fryer to 400°F (204°C) and air fry for 2 minutes. Flip the shrimp and cook for 2 to 4 minutes more, until the flesh turns opaque. 4. Place the romaine in a large bowl and toss with the desired amount of dressing. Top with the shrimp and serve

immediately.

Steamed Tuna with Lemongrass

Preparation time: 10 minutes | Cook time: 10 minutes | Serves 4

- ➢ 4 small tuna steaks
- ➢ 2 tablespoons low-sodium soy sauce
- ➢ 2 teaspoons sesame oil
- ➢ 2 teaspoons rice wine vinegar
- ➢ 1 teaspoon grated peeled fresh ginger
- ➢ ⅛ teaspoon freshly ground black pepper
- ➢ 1 stalk lemongrass, bent in half
- ➢ 3 tablespoons freshly squeezed lemon juice

Instructions

1. Place the tuna steaks on a plate. 2. In a small bowl, whisk the soy sauce, sesame oil, vinegar, and ginger until combined. Pour this mixture over the tuna and gently rub it into both sides. Sprinkle the fish with the pepper. Let marinate for 10 minutes. 3. Insert the crisper plate into the basket and the basket into the unit. Preheat the unit by selecting BAKE, setting the temperature to 390°F (199°C), and setting the time to 3 minutes. Select START/STOP to begin. 4. Once the unit is preheated, place the lemongrass into the basket and top it with the tuna steaks. Drizzle the tuna with the lemon juice and 1 tablespoon of water. 5. Select BAKE, set the temperature to 390°F (199°C), and set the time to 10 minutes. Select START/STOP to begin. 6. When the cooking is complete, a food thermometer inserted into the tuna should register at least 145°F (63°C). Discard the lemongrass and serve the tuna.

Cucumber and Salmon Salad

Preparation time: 10 minutes | Cook time: 8 to 10 minutes | Serves 2

- ➢ 1 pound (454 g) salmon fillet
- ➢ 1½ tablespoons olive oil, divided
- ➢ 1 tablespoon sherry vinegar
- ➢ 1 tablespoon capers, rinsed and drained
- ➢ 1 seedless cucumber, thinly sliced
- ➢ ¼ Vidalia onion, thinly sliced
- ➢ 2 tablespoons chopped fresh parsley
- ➢ Salt and freshly ground black pepper, to taste

Instructions

1. Preheat the air fryer to 400°F (204°C). 2. Lightly coat the salmon with ½ tablespoon of the olive oil. Place skin-side down in the air fryer basket and air fry for 8 to 10 minutes until the fish is opaque and flakes easily with a fork. Transfer the salmon to a plate and let cool to room temperature. Remove the skin and carefully flake the fish into bite-size chunks. 3. In a small bowl, whisk the remaining 1 tablespoon olive oil and the vinegar until thoroughly combined. Add the flaked fish, capers, cucumber, onion, and parsley. Season to taste with salt and freshly ground black pepper. Toss gently to coat. Serve immediately or cover and refrigerate for up to 4 hours.

Balsamic Tilapia

Preparation time: 5 minutes | Cook time: 15 minutes | Serves 4

- ➢ 4 tilapia fillets, boneless
- ➢ 2 tablespoons balsamic vinegar
- ➢ 1 teaspoon avocado oil
- ➢ 1 teaspoon dried basil

Instructions

1. Sprinkle the tilapia fillets with balsamic vinegar, avocado oil, and dried basil. 2. Then put the fillets in the air fryer basket and cook at 365°F (185°C) for 15 minutes.

Tilapia Almondine

Preparation time: 10 minutes | Cook time: 10 minutes | Serves 2

- ➢ ½ cup almond flour or fine dried bread crumbs
- ➢ 2 tablespoons salted butter or ghee, melted
- ➢ 1 teaspoon black pepper
- ➢ ½ teaspoon kosher salt
- ➢ ¼ cup mayonnaise
- ➢ 2 tilapia fillets
- ➢ ½ cup thinly sliced almonds
- ➢ Vegetable oil spray

Instructions

1. In a small bowl, mix together the almond flour, butter, pepper and salt. 2. Spread the mayonnaise on

both sides of each fish fillet. Dredge the fillets in the almond flour mixture. Spread the sliced almonds on one side of each fillet, pressing lightly to adhere. 3. Spray the air fryer basket with vegetable oil spray. Place the fish fillets in the basket. Set the air fryer to 325°F (163°C) for 10 minutes, or until the fish flakes easily with a fork.

Bang Bang Shrimp

Preparation time: 15 minutes | Cook time: 14 minutes | Serves 4

- ➤ Sauce:
- ➤ ½ cup mayonnaise
- ➤ ¼ cup sweet chili sauce
- ➤ 2 to 4 tablespoons Sriracha
- ➤ 1 teaspoon minced fresh ginger
- ➤ Shrimp:
- ➤ 1 pound (454 g) jumbo raw shrimp (21 to 25 count), peeled and deveined
- ➤ 2 tablespoons cornstarch or rice flour
- ➤ ½ teaspoon kosher salt
- ➤ Vegetable oil spray

Instructions

1. For the sauce: In a large bowl, combine the mayonnaise, chili sauce, Sriracha, and ginger. Stir until well combined. Remove half of the sauce to serve as a dipping sauce. 2. For the shrimp: Place the shrimp in a medium bowl. Sprinkle the cornstarch and salt over the shrimp and toss until well coated. 3. Place the shrimp in the air fryer basket in a single layer. (If they won't fit in a single layer, set a rack or trivet on top of the bottom layer of shrimp and place the rest of the shrimp on the rack.) Spray generously with vegetable oil spray. Set the air fryer to 350°F (177°C) for 10 minutes, turning and spraying with additional oil spray halfway through the cooking time. 4. Remove the shrimp and toss in the bowl with half of the sauce. Place the shrimp back in the air fryer basket. Set the air fryer to 350°F (177°C) for an additional 4 to 5 minutes, or until the sauce has formed a glaze. 5. Serve the hot shrimp with the reserved sauce for dipping.

Tuna Casserole

Preparation time: 15 minutes | Cook time: 15 minutes | Serves 4

- ➤ 2 tablespoons salted butter
- ➤ ¼ cup diced white onion
- ➤ ¼ cup chopped white mushrooms
- ➤ 2 stalks celery, finely chopped
- ➤ ½ cup heavy cream
- ➤ ½ cup vegetable broth
- ➤ 2 tablespoons full-fat mayonnaise
- ➤ ¼ teaspoon xanthan gum
- ➤ ½ teaspoon red pepper flakes
- ➤ 2 medium zucchini, spiralized
- ➤ 2 (5 ounces / 142 g) cans albacore tuna
- ➤ 1 ounce (28 g) pork rinds, finely ground

Instructions

1. In a large saucepan over medium heat, melt butter. Add onion, mushrooms, and celery and sauté until fragrant, about 3 to 5 minutes. 2. Pour in heavy cream, vegetable broth, mayonnaise, and xanthan gum. Reduce heat and continue cooking an additional 3 minutes, until the mixture begins to thicken. 3. Add red pepper flakes, zucchini, and tuna. Turn off heat and stir until zucchini noodles are coated. 4. Pour into a round baking dish. Top with ground pork rinds and cover the top of the dish with foil. Place into the air fryer basket. 5. Adjust the temperature to 370°F (188°C) and set the timer for 15 minutes. 6. When 3 minutes remain, remove the foil to brown the top of the casserole. Serve warm.

Salmon Croquettes

Preparation time: 10 minutes | Cook time: 7 to 8 minutes | Serves 4

- ➤ 1 tablespoon oil
- ➤ ½ cup bread crumbs
- ➤ 1 (14¾ -ounce / 418-g) can salmon, drained and all skin and fat removed
- ➤ 1 egg, beaten
- ➤ ⅓ cup coarsely crushed saltine crackers (about 8 crackers)
- ➤ ½ teaspoon Old Bay Seasoning
- ➤ ½ teaspoon onion powder
- ➤ ½ teaspoon Worcestershire sauce

Instructions

1. Preheat the air fryer to 390°F (199°C). 2. In a

shallow dish, mix oil and bread crumbs until crumbly. 3. In a large bowl, combine the salmon, egg, cracker crumbs, Old Bay, onion powder, and Worcestershire. Mix well and shape into 8 small patties about ½-inch thick. 4. Gently dip each patty into bread crumb mixture and turn to coat well on all sides. 5. Cook for 7 to 8 minutes or until outside is crispy and browned.

Shrimp Pasta with Basil and Mushrooms

Preparation time: 10 minutes | Cook time: 10 minutes | Serves 6

- ➤ 1 pound (454 g) small shrimp, peeled and deveined
- ➤ ¼ cup plus 1 tablespoon olive oil, divided
- ➤ ¼ teaspoon garlic powder
- ➤ ¼ teaspoon cayenne
- ➤ 1 pound (454 g) whole grain pasta
- ➤ 5 garlic cloves, minced
- ➤ 8 ounces (227 g) baby bella mushrooms, sliced
- ➤ ½ cup Parmesan, plus more for serving (optional)
- ➤ 1 teaspoon salt
- ➤ ½ teaspoon black pepper
- ➤ ½ cup fresh basil

Instructions

1. Preheat the air fryer to 380°F(193°C). 2. In a small bowl, combine the shrimp, 1 tablespoon olive oil, garlic powder, and cayenne. Toss to coat the shrimp. 3. Place the shrimp into the air fryer basket and roast for 5 minutes. Remove the shrimp and set aside. 4. Cook the pasta according to package directions. Once done cooking, reserve ½ cup pasta water, then drain. 5. Meanwhile, in a large skillet, heat ¼ cup of olive oil over medium heat. Add the garlic and mushrooms and cook down for 5 minutes. 6. Pour the pasta, reserved pasta water, Parmesan, salt, pepper, and basil into the skillet with the vegetable-and-oil mixture, and stir to coat the pasta. 7. Toss in the shrimp and remove from heat, then let the mixture sit for 5 minutes before serving with

additional Parmesan, if desired.

Sole and Cauliflower Fritters

Preparation time: 5 minutes | Cook time: 24 minutes | Serves 2

- ➤ ½ pound (227 g) sole fillets
- ➤ ½ pound (227 g) mashed cauliflower
- ➤ ½ cup red onion, chopped
- ➤ 1 bell pepper, finely chopped
- ➤ 1 egg, beaten
- ➤ 2 garlic cloves, minced
- ➤ 2 tablespoons fresh parsley, chopped
- ➤ 1 tablespoon olive oil
- ➤ 1 tablespoon coconut aminos
- ➤ ½ teaspoon scotch bonnet pepper, minced
- ➤ ½ teaspoon paprika
- ➤ Salt and white pepper, to taste
- ➤ Cooking spray

Instructions

1. Preheat the air fryer to 395°F (202°C). Spray the air fryer basket with cooking spray. 2. Place the sole fillets in the basket and air fry for 10 minutes, flipping them halfway through. 3. When the fillets are done, transfer them to a large bowl. Mash the fillets into flakes. Add the remaining ingredients and stir to combine. 4. Make the fritters: Scoop out 2 tablespoons of the fish mixture and shape into a patty about ½ inch thick with your hands. Repeat with the remaining fish mixture. 5. Arrange the patties in the air fryer basket and bake for 14 minutes, flipping the patties halfway through, or until they are golden brown and cooked through. 6. Cool for 5 minutes and serve on a plate.

Pesto Shrimp with Wild Rice Pilaf

Preparation time: 5 minutes | Cook time: 5 minutes | Serves 4

- ➤ 1 pound (454 g) medium shrimp, peeled and deveined
- ➤ ¼ cup pesto sauce
- ➤ 1 lemon, sliced
- ➤ 2 cups cooked wild rice pilaf

Instructions

1. Preheat the air fryer to 360°F(182°C). 2. In a

medium bowl, toss the shrimp with the pesto sauce until well coated. 3. Place the shrimp in a single layer in the air fryer basket. Put the lemon slices over the shrimp and roast for 5 minutes. 4. Remove the lemons and discard. Serve a quarter of the shrimp over ½ cup wild rice with some favorite steamed vegetables.

Salmon on Bed of Fennel and Carrot

Preparation time: 15 minutes | Cook time: 13 to 14 minutes | Serves 2

> 1 fennel bulb, thinly sliced
> 1 large carrot, peeled and sliced
> 1 small onion, thinly sliced
> ¼ cup low-fat sour cream
> ¼ teaspoon coarsely ground pepper
> 2 (5 ounces / 142 g) salmon fillets

Instructions

1. Combine the fennel, carrot, and onion in a bowl and toss. 2. Put the vegetable mixture into a baking pan. Roast in the air fryer at 400°F (204°C) for 4 minutes or until the vegetables are crisp-tender. 3. Remove the pan from the air fryer. Stir in the sour cream and sprinkle the vegetables with the pepper. 4. Top with the salmon fillets. 5. Return the pan to the air fryer. Roast for another 9 to 10 minutes or until the salmon just barely flakes when tested with a fork.

Lime Lobster Tails

Preparation time: 10 minutes | Cook time: 6 minutes | Serves 4

> 4 lobster tails, peeled
> 2 tablespoons lime juice
> ½ teaspoon dried basil
> ½ teaspoon coconut oil, melted

Instructions

1. Mix lobster tails with lime juice, dried basil, and coconut oil. 2. Put the lobster tails in the air fryer and cook at 380°F (193°C) for 6 minutes.

Crab Cakes

Preparation time: 10 minutes | Cook time: 10 minutes | Serves 4

> 2 (6 ounces / 170 g) cans lump crab meat

> ¼ cup blanched finely ground almond flour
> 1 large egg
> 2 tablespoons full-fat mayonnaise
> ½ teaspoon Dijon mustard
> ½ tablespoon lemon juice
> ½ medium green bell pepper, seeded and chopped
> ¼ cup chopped green onion
> ½ teaspoon Old Bay seasoning

Instructions

1. In a large bowl, combine all ingredients. Form into four balls and flatten into patties. Place patties into the air fryer basket. 2. Adjust the temperature to 350°F (177°C) and air fry for 10 minutes. 3. Flip patties halfway through the cooking time. Serve warm.

Shrimp Curry

Preparation time: 30 minutes | Cook time: 10 minutes | Serves 4

> ¾ cup unsweetened full-fat coconut milk
> ¼ cup finely chopped yellow onion
> 2 teaspoons garam masala
> 1 tablespoon minced fresh ginger
> 1 tablespoon minced garlic
> 1 teaspoon ground turmeric
> 1 teaspoon salt
> ¼ to ½ teaspoon cayenne pepper
> 1 pound (454 g) raw shrimp (21 to 25 count), peeled and deveined
> 2 teaspoons chopped fresh cilantro

Instructions

1. In a large bowl, stir together the coconut milk, onion, garam masala, ginger, garlic, turmeric, salt and cayenne, until well blended. 2. Add the shrimp and toss until coated with sauce on all sides. Marinate at room temperature for 30 minutes. 3. Transfer the shrimp and marinade to a baking pan. Place the pan in the air fryer basket. Set the air fryer to 375°F (191°C) for 10 minutes, stirring halfway through the cooking time. 4. Transfer the shrimp to a serving bowl or platter. Sprinkle with the cilantro

and serve.

Fish Fillets with Lemon-Dill Sauce

Preparation time: 5 minutes | Cook time: 7 minutes | Serves 4

- ➢ 1 pound (454 g) snapper, grouper, or salmon fillets
- ➢ Sea salt and freshly ground black pepper, to taste
- ➢ 1 tablespoon avocado oil
- ➢ ¼ cup sour cream
- ➢ ¼ cup sugar-free mayonnaise
- ➢ 2 tablespoons fresh dill, chopped, plus more for garnish
- ➢ 1 tablespoon freshly squeezed lemon juice
- ➢ ½ teaspoon grated lemon zest

Instructions

1. Pat the fish dry with paper towels and season well with salt and pepper. Brush with the avocado oil. 2. Set the air fryer to 400°F (204°C). Place the fillets in the air fryer basket and air fry for 1 minute. 3. Lower the air fryer temperature to 325°F (163°C) and continue cooking for 5 minutes. Flip the fish and cook for 1 minute more or until an instant-read thermometer reads 145°F (63°C). (If using salmon, cook it to 125°F / 52°C for medium-rare.) 4. While the fish is cooking, make the sauce by combining the sour cream, mayonnaise, dill, lemon juice, and lemon zest in a medium bowl. Season with salt and pepper and stir until combined. Refrigerate until ready to serve. 5. Serve the fish with the sauce, garnished with the remaining dill.

Lemon-Dill Salmon Burgers

Preparation time: 10 minutes | Cook time: 8 minutes | Serves 4

- ➢ 2 (6 ounces / 170 g) fillets of salmon, finely chopped by hand or in a food processor
- ➢ 1 cup fine bread crumbs
- ➢ 1 teaspoon freshly grated lemon zest
- ➢ 2 tablespoons chopped fresh dill weed
- ➢ 1 teaspoon salt
- ➢ Freshly ground black pepper, to taste
- ➢ 2 eggs, lightly beaten
- ➢ 4 brioche or hamburger buns
- ➢ Lettuce, tomato, red onion, avocado, mayonnaise or mustard, for serving

Instructions

1. Preheat the air fryer to 400°F (204°C). 2. Combine all the ingredients in a bowl. Mix together well and divide into four balls. Flatten the balls into patties, making an indentation in the center of each patty with your thumb (this will help the burger stay flat as it cooks) and flattening the sides of the burgers so that they fit nicely into the air fryer basket. 3. Transfer the burgers to the air fryer basket and air fry for 4 minutes. Flip the burgers over and air fry for another 3 to 4 minutes, until nicely browned and firm to the touch. 4. Serve on soft brioche buns with your choice of topping: lettuce, tomato, red onion, avocado, mayonnaise or mustard.

● CHAPTER 7 Snacks and Appetizers

Roasted Grape Dip

Preparation time: 10 minutes | Cook time: 8 to 12 minutes | Serves 6

➢ 2 cups seedless red grapes, rinsed and patted dry
➢ 1 tablespoon apple cider vinegar
➢ 1 tablespoon honey
➢ 1 cup low-fat Greek yogurt
➢ 2 tablespoons 2% milk
➢ 2 tablespoons minced fresh basil

Instructions

1. In the air fryer basket, sprinkle the grapes with the cider vinegar and drizzle with the honey. Toss to coat. Roast the grapes at 380°F (193°C) for 8 to 12 minutes, or until shriveled but still soft. Remove from the air fryer. 2. In a medium bowl, stir together the yogurt and milk. 3. Gently blend in the grapes and basil. Serve immediately, or cover and chill for 1 to 2 hours.

Goat Cheese and Garlic Crostini

Preparation time: 3 minutes | Cook time: 5 minutes | Serves 4

➢ 1 whole wheat baguette
➢ ¼ cup olive oil
➢ 2 garlic cloves, minced
➢ 4 ounces (113 g) goat cheese
➢ 2 tablespoons fresh basil, minced

Instructions

1. Preheat the air fryer to 380°F(193°C). 2. Cut the baguette into ½-inch-thick slices. 3. In a small bowl, mix together the olive oil and garlic, then brush it over one side of each slice of bread. 4. Place the olive-oil-coated bread in a single layer in the air fryer basket and bake for 5 minutes. 5. Meanwhile, in a small bowl, mix together the goat cheese and basil. 6. Remove the toast from the air fryer, then spread a thin layer of the goat cheese mixture over the top of each piece and serve.

Bacon-Wrapped Pickle Spears

Preparation time: 10 minutes | Cook time: 8 minutes | Serves 4

➢ 8 to 12 slices bacon
➢ ¼ cup (2 ounces / 57 g) cream cheese, softened
➢ ¼ cup shredded Mozzarella cheese
➢ 8 dill pickle spears
➢ ½ cup ranch dressing

Instructions

1. Lay the bacon slices on a flat surface. In a medium bowl, combine the cream cheese and Mozzarella. Stir until well blended. Spread the cheese mixture over the bacon slices. 2. Place a pickle spear on a bacon slice and roll the bacon around the pickle in a spiral, ensuring the pickle is fully covered. (You may need to use more than one slice of bacon per pickle to fully cover the spear.) Tuck in the ends to ensure the bacon stays put. Repeat to wrap all the pickles. 3. Place the wrapped pickles in the air fryer basket in a single layer. Set the air fryer to 400°F (204°C) for 8 minutes, or until the bacon is cooked through and crisp on the edges. 4. Serve the pickle spears with ranch dressing on the side.

Baked Spanakopita Dip

Preparation time: 10 minutes | Cook time: 15 minutes | Serves 2

➢ Olive oil cooking spray
➢ 3 tablespoons olive oil, divided
➢ 2 tablespoons minced white onion
➢ 2 garlic cloves, minced
➢ 4 cups fresh spinach
➢ 4 ounces (113 g) cream cheese, softened
➢ 4 ounces (113 g) feta cheese, divided
➢ Zest of 1 lemon
➢ ¼ teaspoon ground nutmeg
➢ 1 teaspoon dried dill
➢ ½ teaspoon salt

> Pita chips, carrot sticks, or sliced bread for serving (optional)

Instructions

1. Preheat the air fryer to 360°F(182°C). Coat the inside of a 6-inch ramekin or baking dish with olive oil cooking spray. 2. In a large skillet over medium heat, heat 1 tablespoon of the olive oil. Add the onion, then cook for 1 minute. 3. Add in the garlic and cook, stirring for 1 minute more. 4. Reduce the heat to low and mix in the spinach and water. Let this cook for 2 to 3 minutes, or until the spinach has wilted. Remove the skillet from the heat. 5. In a medium bowl, combine the cream cheese, 2 ounces (57 g) of the feta, and the remaining 2 tablespoons of olive oil, along with the lemon zest, nutmeg, dill, and salt. Mix until just combined. 6. Add the vegetables to the cheese base and stir until combined. 7. Pour the dip mixture into the prepared ramekin and top with the remaining 2 ounces (57 g) of feta cheese. 8. Place the dip into the air fryer basket and cook for 10 minutes, or until heated through and bubbling. 9. Serve with pita chips, carrot sticks, or sliced bread.

Spicy Chicken Bites

Preparation time: 10 minutes | Cook time: 10 to 12 minutes | Makes 30 bites

> 8 ounces boneless and skinless chicken thighs, cut into 30 pieces
> ¼ teaspoon kosher salt
> 2 tablespoons hot sauce
> Cooking spray

Instructions

1. Preheat the air fryer to 390°F (199°C). 2. Spray the air fryer basket with cooking spray and season the chicken bites with the kosher salt, then place in the basket and air fry for 10 to 12 minutes or until crispy. 3. While the chicken bites cook, pour the hot sauce into a large bowl. 4. Remove the bites and add to the sauce bowl, tossing to coat. Serve warm.

Crispy Breaded Beef Cubes

Preparation time: 10 minutes | Cook time: 12 to 16 minutes | Serves 4

> 1 pound (454 g) sirloin tip, cut into 1-inch cubes

> 1 cup cheese pasta sauce
> 1½ cups soft bread crumbs
> 2 tablespoons olive oil
> ½ teaspoon dried marjoram

Instructions

1. Preheat the air fryer to 360°F (182°C). 2. In a medium bowl, toss the beef with the pasta sauce to coat. 3. In a shallow bowl, combine the bread crumbs, oil, and marjoram, and mix well. Drop the beef cubes, one at a time, into the bread crumb mixture to coat thoroughly. 4. Air fry the beef in two batches for 6 to 8 minutes, shaking the basket once during cooking time, until the beef is at least 145°F (63°C) and the outside is crisp and brown. 5. Serve hot.

Greek Potato Skins with Olives and Feta

Preparation time: 5 minutes | Cook time: 45 minutes | Serves 4

> 2 russet potatoes
> 3 tablespoons olive oil, divided, plus more for drizzling (optional)
> 1 teaspoon kosher salt, divided
> ¼ teaspoon black pepper
> 2 tablespoons fresh cilantro, chopped, plus more for serving
> ¼ cup Kalamata olives, diced
> ¼ cup crumbled feta
> Chopped fresh parsley, for garnish (optional)

Instructions

1. Preheat the air fryer to 380°F(193°C). 2. Using a fork, poke 2 to 3 holes in the potatoes, then coat each with about ½ tablespoon olive oil and ½ teaspoon salt. 3. Place the potatoes into the air fryer basket and bake for 30 minutes. 4. Remove the potatoes from the air fryer, and slice in half. Using a spoon, scoop out the flesh of the potatoes, leaving a ½-inch layer of potato inside the skins, and set the skins aside. 5. In a medium bowl, combine the scooped potato middles with the remaining 2 tablespoons of olive oil, ½ teaspoon of salt, black pepper, and cilantro. Mix until well combined. 6. Divide the potato filling into the now-empty potato skins,

spreading it evenly over them. Top each potato with a tablespoon each of the olives and feta. 7. Place the loaded potato skins back into the air fryer and bake for 15 minutes. 8. Serve with additional chopped cilantro or parsley and a drizzle of olive oil, if desired.

Greek Street Tacos

Preparation time: 10 minutes | Cook time: 3 minutes | Makes 8 small tacos

- 8 small flour tortillas (4-inch diameter)
- 8 tablespoons hummus
- 4 tablespoons crumbled feta cheese
- 4 tablespoons chopped kalamata or other olives (optional)
- Olive oil for misting

Instructions

1. Place 1 tablespoon of hummus or tapenade in the center of each tortilla. Top with 1 teaspoon of feta crumbles and 1 teaspoon of chopped olives, if using. 2. Using your finger or a small spoon, moisten the edges of the tortilla all around with water. 3. Fold tortilla over to make a half-moon shape. Press center gently. Then press the edges firmly to seal in the filling. 4. Mist both sides with olive oil. 5. Place in air fryer basket very close but try not to overlap. 6. Air fry at 390°F (199°C) for 3 minutes, just until lightly browned and crispy.

Onion Pakoras

Preparation time: 30 minutes | Cook time: 10 minutes per batch | Serves 2

- 2 medium yellow or white onions, sliced (2 cups)
- ½ cup chopped fresh cilantro
- 2 tablespoons vegetable oil
- 1 tablespoon chickpea flour
- 1 tablespoon rice flour, or 2 tablespoons chickpea flour
- 1 teaspoon ground turmeric
- 1 teaspoon cumin seeds
- 1 teaspoon kosher salt
- ½ teaspoon cayenne pepper
- Vegetable oil spray

Instructions

1. In a large bowl, combine the onions, cilantro, oil, chickpea flour, rice flour, turmeric, cumin seeds, salt, and cayenne. Stir to combine. Cover and let stand for 30 minutes or up to overnight. (This allows the onions to release moisture, creating a batter.) Mix well before using. 2. Spray the air fryer basket generously with vegetable oil spray. Drop half of the batter in 6 heaping tablespoons into the basket. Set the air fryer to 350°F (177°C) for 8 minutes. Carefully turn the pakoras over and spray with oil spray. Set the air fryer for 2 minutes, or until the batter is cooked through and crisp. 3. Repeat with remaining batter to make 6 more pakoras, checking at 6 minutes for doneness. Serve hot.

Roasted Mushrooms with Garlic

Preparation time: 3 minutes | Cook time: 22 to 27 minutes | Serves 4

- 16 garlic cloves, peeled
- 2 teaspoons olive oil, divided
- 16 button mushrooms
- ½ teaspoon dried marjoram
- ⅛ teaspoon freshly ground black pepper
- 1 tablespoon white wine or low-sodium vegetable broth

Instructions

1. In a baking pan, mix the garlic with 1 teaspoon of olive oil. Roast in the air fryer at 350°F (177°C) for 12 minutes. 2. Add the mushrooms, marjoram, and pepper. Stir to coat. Drizzle with the remaining 1 teaspoon of olive oil and the white wine. 3. Return to the air fryer and roast for 10 to 15 minutes more, or until the mushrooms and garlic cloves are tender. Serve.

Sweet Potato Fries with Mayonnaise

Preparation time: 5 minutes | Cook time: 20 minutes | Serves 2 to 3

- 1 large sweet potato (about 1 pound / 454 g), scrubbed
- 1 teaspoon vegetable or canola oil
- Salt, to taste
- Dipping Sauce:

- ➤ ¼ cup light mayonnaise
- ➤ ½ teaspoon sriracha sauce
- ➤ 1 tablespoon spicy brown mustard
- ➤ 1 tablespoon sweet Thai chili sauce

Instructions

1. Preheat the air fryer to 200°F (93°C). 2. On a flat work surface, cut the sweet potato into fry-shaped strips about ¼ inch wide and ¼ inch thick. You can use a mandoline to slice the sweet potato quickly and uniformly. 3. In a medium bowl, drizzle the sweet potato strips with the oil and toss well. 4. Transfer to the air fryer basket and air fry for 10 minutes, shaking the basket twice during cooking. 5. Remove the air fryer basket and sprinkle with the salt and toss to coat. 6. Increase the air fryer temperature to 400°F (204°C) and air fry for an additional 10 minutes, or until the fries are crispy and tender. Shake the basket a few times during cooking. 7. Meanwhile, whisk together all the ingredients for the sauce in a small bowl. 8. Remove the sweet potato fries from the basket to a plate and serve warm alongside the dipping sauce.

Pepperoni Pizza Dip

Preparation time: 10 minutes | Cook time: 10 minutes | Serves 6

- ➤ 6 ounces (170 g) cream cheese, softened
- ➤ ¾ cup shredded Italian cheese blend
- ➤ ¼ cup sour cream
- ➤ 1½ teaspoons dried Italian seasoning
- ➤ ¼ teaspoon garlic salt
- ➤ ¼ teaspoon onion powder
- ➤ ¾ cup pizza sauce
- ➤ ½ cup sliced miniature pepperoni
- ➤ ¼ cup sliced black olives
- ➤ 1 tablespoon thinly sliced green onion

Cut-up raw vegetables, toasted baguette slices, pita chips, or tortilla chips, for serving

Instructions

1. In a small bowl, combine the cream cheese, ¼ cup of the shredded cheese, the sour cream, Italian seasoning, garlic salt, and onion powder. Stir until smooth and the ingredients are well blended. 2.

Spread the mixture in a baking pan. Top with the pizza sauce, spreading to the edges. Sprinkle with the remaining ½ cup shredded cheese. Arrange the pepperoni slices on top of the cheese. Top with the black olives and green onion. 3. Place the pan in the air fryer basket. Set the air fryer to 350°F (177°C) for 10 minutes, or until the pepperoni is beginning to brown on the edges and the cheese is bubbly and lightly browned. 4. Let stand for 5 minutes before serving with vegetables, toasted baguette slices, pita chips, or tortilla chips.

Cheese Drops

Preparation time: 15 minutes | Cook time: 10 minutes per batch | Serves 8

- ➤ ¾ cup all-purpose flour
- ➤ ½ teaspoon kosher salt
- ➤ ¼ teaspoon cayenne pepper
- ➤ ¼ teaspoon smoked paprika
- ➤ ¼ teaspoon black pepper
- ➤ Dash garlic powder (optional)
- ➤ ¼ cup butter, softened
- ➤ 1 cup shredded sharp Cheddar cheese, at room temperature
- ➤ Olive oil spray

Instructions

1. In a small bowl, combine the flour, salt, cayenne, paprika, pepper, and garlic powder, if using. 2. Using a food processor, cream the butter and cheese until smooth. Gently add the seasoned flour and process until the dough is well combined, smooth, and no longer sticky. (Or make the dough in a stand mixer fitted with the paddle attachment: Cream the butter and cheese on medium speed until smooth, then add the seasoned flour and beat at low speed until smooth.) 3. Divide the dough into 32 equal-size pieces. On a lightly floured surface, roll each piece into a small ball. 4. Spray the air fryer basket with oil spray. Arrange 16 cheese drops in the basket. Set the air fryer to 325°F (163°C) for 10 minutes, or until drops are just starting to brown. Transfer to a wire rack. Repeat with remaining dough, checking for doneness at 8 minutes. 5. Cool the cheese drops completely on the wire rack. Store in an airtight

container until ready to serve, or up to 1 or 2 days.

Veggie Salmon Nachos

Preparation time: 10 minutes | Cook time: 9 to 12 minutes | Serves 6

- 2 ounces (57 g) baked no-salt corn tortilla chips
- 1 (5 ounces / 142 g) baked salmon fillet, flaked
- ½ cup canned low-sodium black beans, rinsed and drained
- 1 red bell pepper, chopped
- ½ cup grated carrot
- 1 jalapeño pepper, minced
- ⅓ cup shredded low-sodium low-fat Swiss cheese
- 1 tomato, chopped

Instructions

1. Preheat the air fryer to 360ºF (182ºC). 2. In a baking pan, layer the tortilla chips. Top with the salmon, black beans, red bell pepper, carrot, jalapeño, and Swiss cheese. 3. Bake in the air fryer for 9 to 12 minutes, or until the cheese is melted and starts to brown. 4. Top with the tomato and serve.

Bruschetta with Basil Pesto

Preparation time: 10 minutes | Cook time: 5 to 11 minutes | Serves 4

- 8 slices French bread, ½ inch thick
- 2 tablespoons softened butter
- 1 cup shredded Mozzarella cheese
- ½ cup basil pesto
- 1 cup chopped grape tomatoes
- 2 green onions, thinly sliced

Instructions

1. Preheat the air fryer to 350ºF (177ºC). 2. Spread the bread with the butter and place butter-side up in the air fryer basket. Bake for 3 to 5 minutes, or until the bread is light golden brown. 3. Remove the bread from the basket and top each piece with some of the cheese. Return to the basket in 2 batches and bake for 1 to 3 minutes, or until the cheese melts. 4. Meanwhile, combine the pesto, tomatoes, and green onions in a small bowl. 5. When the cheese has melted, remove the bread from the air fryer and place on a serving plate. Top each slice with some of the pesto mixture and serve.

String Bean Fries

Preparation time: 15 minutes | Cook time: 5 to 6 minutes | Serves 4

- ½ pound (227 g) fresh string beans
- 2 eggs
- 4 teaspoons water
- ½ cup white flour
- ½ cup bread crumbs
- ¼ teaspoon salt
- ¼ teaspoon ground black pepper
- ¼ teaspoon dry mustard (optional)
- Oil for misting or cooking spray

Instructions

1. Preheat the air fryer to 360ºF (182ºC). 2. Trim stem ends from string beans, wash, and pat dry. 3. In a shallow dish, beat eggs and water together until well blended. 4. Place flour in a second shallow dish. 5. In a third shallow dish, stir together the bread crumbs, salt, pepper, and dry mustard if using. 6. Dip each string bean in egg mixture, flour, egg mixture again, then bread crumbs. 7. When you finish coating all the string beans, open air fryer and place them in basket. 8. Cook for 3 minutes. 9. Stop and mist string beans with oil or cooking spray. 10. Cook for 2 to 3 more minutes or until string beans are crispy and nicely browned.

Parmesan French Fries

Preparation time: 10 minutes | Cook time: 25 minutes | Serves 2 to 3

- 2 to 3 large russet potatoes, peeled and cut into ½-inch sticks
- 2 teaspoons vegetable or canola oil
- ¾ cup grated Parmesan cheese
- ½ teaspoon salt
- Freshly ground black pepper, to taste
- 1 teaspoon fresh chopped parsley

Instructions

1. Bring a large saucepan of salted water to a boil on the stovetop while you peel and cut the potatoes. Blanch the potatoes in the boiling salted water for 4 minutes while you preheat the air fryer to 400ºF

(204ºC). Strain the potatoes and rinse them with cold water. Dry them well with a clean kitchen towel. 2. Toss the dried potato sticks gently with the oil and place them in the air fryer basket. Air fry for 25 minutes, shaking the basket a few times while the fries cook to help them brown evenly. 3. Combine the Parmesan cheese, salt and pepper. With 2 minutes left on the air fryer cooking time, sprinkle the fries with the Parmesan cheese mixture. Toss the fries to coat them evenly with the cheese mixture and continue to air fry for the final 2 minutes, until the cheese has melted and just starts to brown. Sprinkle the finished fries with chopped parsley, a little more grated Parmesan cheese if you like, and serve.

Ranch Oyster Snack Crackers

Preparation time: 3 minutes | Cook time: 12 minutes | Serves 6

- ➤ Oil, for spraying
- ➤ ¼ cup olive oil
- ➤ 2 teaspoons dry ranch seasoning
- ➤ 1 teaspoon chili powder
- ➤ ½ teaspoon dried dill
- ➤ ½ teaspoon granulated garlic
- ➤ ½ teaspoon salt
- ➤ 1 (9 ounces / 255 g) bag oyster crackers

Instructions

1. Preheat the air fryer to 325ºF (163ºC). Line the air fryer basket with parchment and spray lightly with oil. 2. In a large bowl, mix together the olive oil, ranch seasoning, chili powder, dill, garlic, and salt. Add the crackers and toss until evenly coated. 3. Place the mixture in the prepared basket. 4. Cook for 10 to 12 minutes, shaking or stirring every 3 to 4 minutes, or until crisp and golden brown.

Garlic Edamame

Preparation time: 5 minutes | Cook time: 10 minutes | Serves 4

- ➤ Olive oil
- ➤ 1 (16-ounce / 454-g) bag frozen edamame in pods
- ➤ ½ teaspoon salt
- ➤ ½ teaspoon garlic salt
- ➤ ¼ teaspoon freshly ground black pepper

- ➤ ½ teaspoon red pepper flakes (optional)

Instructions

1. Spray the air fryer basket lightly with olive oil. 2. In a medium bowl, add the frozen edamame and lightly spray with olive oil. Toss to coat. 3. In a small bowl, mix together the salt, garlic salt, black pepper, and red pepper flakes (if using). Add the mixture to the edamame and toss until evenly coated. 4. Place half the edamame in the air fryer basket. Do not overfill the basket. 5. Air fry at 375ºF (191ºC) for 5 minutes. Shake the basket and cook until the edamame is starting to brown and get crispy, 3 to 5 more minutes. 6. Repeat with the remaining edamame and serve immediately.

Homemade Sweet Potato Chips

Preparation time: 5 minutes | Cook time: 15 minutes | Serves 2

- ➤ 1 large sweet potato, sliced thin
- ➤ ⅛ teaspoon salt
- ➤ 2 tablespoons olive oil

Instructions

1. Preheat the air fryer to 380ºF(193ºC). 2. In a small bowl, toss the sweet potatoes, salt, and olive oil together until the potatoes are well coated. 3. Put the sweet potato slices into the air fryer and spread them out in a single layer. 4. Fry for 10 minutes. Stir, then air fry for 3 to 5 minutes more, or until the chips reach the preferred level of crispiness.

Grilled Ham and Cheese on Raisin Bread

Preparation time: 5 minutes | Cook time: 10 minutes | Serves 1

- ➤ 2 slices raisin bread
- ➤ 2 tablespoons butter, softened
- ➤ 2 teaspoons honey mustard
- ➤ 3 slices thinly sliced honey ham (about 3 ounces / 85 g)
- ➤ 4 slices Muenster cheese (about 3 ounces / 85 g)
- ➤ 2 toothpicks

Instructions

1. Preheat the air fryer to 370ºF (188ºC). 2. Spread

the softened butter on one side of both slices of raisin bread and place the bread, buttered side down on the counter. Spread the honey mustard on the other side of each slice of bread. Layer 2 slices of cheese, the ham and the remaining 2 slices of cheese on one slice of bread and top with the other slice of bread. Remember to leave the buttered side of the bread on the outside. 3. Transfer the sandwich to the air fryer basket and secure the sandwich with toothpicks. 4. Air fry for 5 minutes. Flip the sandwich over, remove the toothpicks and air fry for another 5 minutes. Cut the sandwich in half and enjoy!

Rumaki

Preparation time: 30 minutes | Cook time: 10 to 12 minutes per batch | Makes about 24 rumaki

- ➢ 10 ounces (283 g) raw chicken livers
- ➢ 1 can sliced water chestnuts, drained
- ➢ ¼ cup low-sodium teriyaki sauce

12 slices turkey bacon

Instructions

1. Cut livers into 1½-inch pieces, trimming out tough veins as you slice. 2. Place livers, water chestnuts, and teriyaki sauce in small container with lid. If needed, add another tablespoon of teriyaki sauce to make sure livers are covered. Refrigerate for 1 hour. 3. When ready to cook, cut bacon slices in half crosswise. 4. Wrap 1 piece of liver and 1 slice of water chestnut in each bacon strip. Secure with toothpick. 5. When you have wrapped half of the livers, place them in the air fryer basket in a single layer. 6. Air fry at 390°F (199°C) for 10 to 12 minutes, until liver is done and bacon is crispy. 7. While first batch cooks, wrap the remaining livers. Repeat step 6 to cook your second batch.

Rosemary-Garlic Shoestring Fries

Preparation time: 5 minutes | Cook time: 18 minutes | Serves 2

- ➢ 1 large russet potato (about 12 ounces / 340 g), scrubbed clean, and julienned
- ➢ 1 tablespoon vegetable oil
- ➢ Leaves from 1 sprig fresh rosemary

- ➢ Kosher salt and freshly ground black pepper, to taste
- ➢ 1 garlic clove, thinly sliced
- ➢ Flaky sea salt, for serving

Instructions

1. Preheat the air fryer to 400°F (204°C). 2. Place the julienned potatoes in a large colander and rinse under cold running water until the water runs clear. Spread the potatoes out on a double-thick layer of paper towels and pat dry. 3. In a large bowl, combine the potatoes, oil, and rosemary. Season with kosher salt and pepper and toss to coat evenly. Place the potatoes in the air fryer and air fry for 18 minutes, shaking the basket every 5 minutes and adding the garlic in the last 5 minutes of cooking, or until the fries are golden brown and crisp. 4. Transfer the fries to a plate and sprinkle with flaky sea salt while they're hot. Serve immediately.

Feta and Quinoa Stuffed Mushrooms

Preparation time: 5 minutes | Cook time: 8 minutes | Serves 6

- ➢ 2 tablespoons finely diced red bell pepper
- ➢ 1 garlic clove, minced
- ➢ ¼ cup cooked quinoa
- ➢ ⅛ teaspoon salt
- ➢ ¼ teaspoon dried oregano
- ➢ 24 button mushrooms, stemmed
- ➢ 2 ounces (57 g) crumbled feta
- ➢ 3 tablespoons whole wheat bread crumbs
- ➢ Olive oil cooking spray

Instructions

1. Preheat the air fryer to 360°F(182°C). 2. In a small bowl, combine the bell pepper, garlic, quinoa, salt, and oregano. 3. Spoon the quinoa stuffing into the mushroom caps until just filled. 4. Add a small piece of feta to the top of each mushroom. 5. Sprinkle a pinch bread crumbs over the feta on each mushroom. 6. Spray the basket of the air fryer with olive oil cooking spray, then gently place the mushrooms into the basket, making sure that they don't touch each

other. (Depending on the size of the air fryer, you may have to cook them in two batches.) 7. Place the basket into the air fryer and bake for 8 minutes. 8. Remove from the air fryer and serve.

Kale Chips with Sesame

Preparation time: 15 minutes | Cook time: 8 minutes | Serves 5

- ➤ 8 cups deribbed kale leaves, torn into 2-inch pieces
- ➤ 1½ tablespoons olive oil
- ➤ ¾ teaspoon chili powder
- ➤ ¼ teaspoon garlic powder
- ➤ ½ teaspoon paprika
- ➤ 2 teaspoons sesame seeds

Instructions

1. Preheat air fryer to 350°F (177°C). 2. In a large bowl, toss the kale with the olive oil, chili powder, garlic powder, paprika, and sesame seeds until well coated. 3. Put the kale in the air fryer basket and air fry for 8 minutes, flipping the kale twice during cooking, or until the kale is crispy. 4. Serve warm.

Veggie Shrimp Toast

Preparation time: 15 minutes | Cook time: 3 to 6 minutes | Serves 4

- ➤ 8 large raw shrimp, peeled and finely chopped
- ➤ 1 egg white
- ➤ 2 garlic cloves, minced
- ➤ 3 tablespoons minced red bell pepper
- ➤ 1 medium celery stalk, minced
- ➤ 2 tablespoons cornstarch
- ➤ ¼ teaspoon Chinese five-spice powder
- ➤ 3 slices firm thin-sliced no-sodium whole-wheat bread

Instructions

1. Preheat the air fryer to 350°F (177°C). 2. In a small bowl, stir together the shrimp, egg white, garlic, red bell pepper, celery, cornstarch, and five-spice powder. Top each slice of bread with one-third of the shrimp mixture, spreading it evenly to the edges. With a sharp knife, cut each slice of bread into 4 strips. 3. Place the shrimp toasts in the air fryer basket in a single layer. You may need to cook them

in batches. Air fry for 3 to 6 minutes, until crisp and golden brown. 4. Serve hot.

Air Fried Pot Stickers

Preparation time: 10 minutes | Cook time: 18 to 20 minutes | Makes 30 pot stickers

- ➤ ½ cup finely chopped cabbage
- ➤ ¼ cup finely chopped red bell pepper
- ➤ 2 green onions, finely chopped
- ➤ 1 egg, beaten
- ➤ 2 tablespoons cocktail sauce
- ➤ 2 teaspoons low-sodium soy sauce
- ➤ 30 wonton wrappers
- ➤ 1 tablespoon water, for brushing the wrappers

Instructions

1. Preheat the air fryer to 360°F (182°C). 2. In a small bowl, combine the cabbage, pepper, green onions, egg, cocktail sauce, and soy sauce, and mix well. 3. Put about 1 teaspoon of the mixture in the center of each wonton wrapper. Fold the wrapper in half, covering the filling; dampen the edges with water, and seal. You can crimp the edges of the wrapper with your fingers so they look like the pot stickers you get in restaurants. Brush them with water. 4. Place the pot stickers in the air fryer basket and air fry in 2 batches for 9 to 10 minutes, or until the pot stickers are hot and the bottoms are lightly browned. 5. Serve hot.

Fried Peaches

Preparation time: 15 minutes | Cook time: 6 to 8 minutes | Serves 4

- ➤ 2 egg whites
- ➤ 1 tablespoon water
- ➤ ¼ cup sliced almonds
- ➤ 2 tablespoons brown sugar
- ➤ ½ teaspoon almond extract
- ➤ 1 cup crisp rice cereal
- ➤ 2 medium, very firm peaches, peeled and pitted
- ➤ ¼ cup cornstarch
- ➤ Oil for misting or cooking spray

Instructions

1. Preheat the air fryer to 390°F (199°C). 2. Beat together egg whites and water in a shallow dish. 3. In a food processor, combine the almonds, brown sugar, and almond extract. Process until ingredients combine well and the nuts are finely chopped. 4. Add cereal and pulse just until cereal crushes. Pour crumb mixture into a shallow dish or onto a plate. 5. Cut each peach into eighths and place in a plastic bag or container with lid. Add cornstarch, seal, and shake to coat. 6. Remove peach slices from bag or container, tapping them hard to shake off the excess cornstarch. Dip in egg wash and roll in crumbs. Spray with oil. 7. Place in air fryer basket and cook for 5 minutes. Shake basket, separate any that have stuck together, and spritz a little oil on any spots that aren't browning. 8. Cook for 1 to 3 minutes longer, until golden brown and crispy.

Crunchy Chickpeas

Preparation time: 5 minutes | Cook time: 15 to 20 minutes | Serves 4

➢ ½ teaspoon chili powder
➢ ½ teaspoon ground cumin
➢ ¼ teaspoon cayenne pepper
➢ ¼ teaspoon salt
➢ 1 (19 ounces / 539 g) can chickpeas, drained and rinsed
➢ Cooking spray

Instructions

1. Preheat the air fryer to 390°F (199°C). Lightly spritz the air fryer basket with cooking spray. 2. Mix the chili powder, cumin, cayenne pepper, and salt in a small bowl. 3. Place the chickpeas in a medium bowl and lightly mist with cooking spray. 4. Add the spice mixture to the chickpeas and toss until evenly coated. 5. Place the chickpeas in the air fryer basket and air fry for 15 to 20 minutes, or until the chickpeas are cooked to your preferred crunchiness. Shake the basket three or four times during cooking. 6. Let the chickpeas cool for 5 minutes before serving.

Peppery Chicken Meatballs

Preparation time: 5 minutes | Cook time: 13 to 20 minutes | Makes 16 meatballs

➢ 2 teaspoons olive oil
➢ ¼ cup minced onion
➢ ¼ cup minced red bell pepper
➢ 2 vanilla wafers, crushed
➢ 1 egg white
➢ ½ teaspoon dried thyme
➢ ½ pound (227 g) ground chicken breast

Instructions

1. Preheat the air fryer to 370°F (188°C). 2. In a baking pan, mix the olive oil, onion, and red bell pepper. Put the pan in the air fryer. Air fry for 3 to 5 minutes, or until the vegetables are tender. 3. In a medium bowl, mix the cooked vegetables, crushed wafers, egg white, and thyme until well combined 4. Mix in the chicken, gently but thoroughly, until everything is combined. 5. Form the mixture into 16 meatballs and place them in the air fryer basket. Air fry for 10 to 15 minutes, or until the meatballs reach an internal temperature of 165°F (74°C) on a meat thermometer. 6. Serve immediately.

● CHAPTER 8 Vegetables and Sides

Sesame-Ginger Broccoli

Preparation time: 10 minutes | Cook time: 15 minutes | Serves 4

- 3 tablespoons toasted sesame oil
- 2 teaspoons sesame seeds
- 1 tablespoon chili-garlic sauce
- 2 teaspoons minced fresh ginger
- ½ teaspoon kosher salt
- ½ teaspoon black pepper
- 1 (16-ounce / 454-g) package frozen broccoli florets (do not thaw)

Instructions

1. In a large bowl, combine the sesame oil, sesame seeds, chili-garlic sauce, ginger, salt, and pepper. Stir until well combined. Add the broccoli and toss until well coated. 2. Arrange the broccoli in the air fryer basket. Set the air fryer to 325ºF (163ºC) for 15 minutes, or until the broccoli is crisp, tender, and the edges are lightly browned, gently tossing halfway through the cooking time.

Cauliflower Steaks Gratin

Preparation time: 10 minutes | Cook time: 13 minutes | Serves 2

- 1 head cauliflower
- 1 tablespoon olive oil
- Salt and freshly ground black pepper, to taste
- ½ teaspoon chopped fresh thyme leaves
- 3 tablespoons grated Parmigiano-Reggiano cheese
- 2 tablespoons panko bread crumbs

Instructions

1. Preheat the air fryer to 370ºF (188ºC). 2. Cut two steaks out of the center of the cauliflower. To do this, cut the cauliflower in half and then cut one slice about 1-inch thick off each half. The rest of the cauliflower will fall apart into florets, which you can roast on their own or save for another meal. 3. Brush both sides of the cauliflower steaks with olive oil and season with salt, freshly ground black pepper and fresh thyme. Place the cauliflower steaks into the air fryer basket and air fry for 6 minutes. Turn the steaks over and air fry for another 4 minutes. Combine the Parmesan cheese and panko bread crumbs and sprinkle the mixture over the tops of both steaks and air fry for another 3 minutes until the cheese has melted and the bread crumbs have browned. Serve this with some sautéed bitter greens and air-fried blistered tomatoes.

Roasted Salsa

Preparation time: 15 minutes | Cook time: 30 minutes | Makes 2 cups

- 2 large San Marzano tomatoes, cored and cut into large chunks
- ½ medium white onion, peeled and large-diced
- ½ medium jalapeño, seeded and large-diced
- 2 cloves garlic, peeled and diced
- ½ teaspoon salt
- 1 tablespoon coconut oil
- ¼ cup fresh lime juice

Instructions

1. Place tomatoes, onion, and jalapeño into an ungreased round nonstick baking dish. Add garlic, then sprinkle with salt and drizzle with coconut oil. 2. Place dish into air fryer basket. Adjust the temperature to 300ºF (149ºC) and bake for 30 minutes. Vegetables will be dark brown around the edges and tender when done. 3. Pour mixture into a food processor or blender. Add lime juice. Process on low speed 30 seconds until only a few chunks remain. 4. Transfer salsa to a sealable container and refrigerate at least 1 hour. Serve chilled.

Fried Asparagus

Preparation time: 5 minutes | Cook

time: 12 minutes | Serves 4
- ➢ 1 tablespoon olive oil
- ➢ 1 pound (454 g) asparagus spears, ends trimmed
- ➢ ¼ teaspoon salt
- ➢ ¼ teaspoon ground black pepper
- ➢ 1 tablespoon salted butter, melted

Instructions

1. In a large bowl, drizzle olive oil over asparagus spears and sprinkle with salt and pepper. 2. Place spears into ungreased air fryer basket. Adjust the temperature to 375°F (191°C) and set the timer for 12 minutes, shaking the basket halfway through cooking. Asparagus will be lightly browned and tender when done. 3. Transfer to a large dish and drizzle with butter. Serve warm.

Garlic and Thyme Tomatoes

Preparation time: 10 minutes | Cook time: 15 minutes | Serves 2 to 4
- ➢ 4 Roma tomatoes
- ➢ 1 tablespoon olive oil
- ➢ Salt and freshly ground black pepper, to taste
- ➢ 1 clove garlic, minced
- ➢ ½ teaspoon dried thyme

Instructions

1. Preheat the air fryer to 390°F (199°C). 2. Cut the tomatoes in half and scoop out the seeds and any pithy parts with your fingers. Place the tomatoes in a bowl and toss with the olive oil, salt, pepper, garlic and thyme. 3. Transfer the tomatoes to the air fryer, cut side up. Air fry for 15 minutes. The edges should just start to brown. Let the tomatoes cool to an edible temperature for a few minutes and then use in pastas, on top of crostini, or as an accompaniment to any poultry, meat or fish.

Cheese-Walnut Stuffed Mushrooms

Preparation time: 5 minutes | Cook time: 10 minutes | Serves 4
- ➢ 4 large portobello mushrooms
- ➢ 1 tablespoon canola oil

- ➢ ½ cup shredded Mozzarella cheese
- ➢ ⅓ cup minced walnuts
- ➢ 2 tablespoons chopped fresh parsley
- ➢ Cooking spray

Instructions

1. Preheat the air fryer to 350°F (177°C). Spritz the air fryer basket with cooking spray. 2. On a clean work surface, remove the mushroom stems. Scoop out the gills with a spoon and discard. Coat the mushrooms with canola oil. Top each mushroom evenly with the shredded Mozzarella cheese, followed by the minced walnuts. 3. Arrange the mushrooms in the air fryer and roast for 10 minutes until golden brown. 4. Transfer the mushrooms to a plate and sprinkle the parsley on top for garnish before serving.

Saltine Wax Beans

Preparation time: 10 minutes | Cook time: 7 minutes | Serves 4
- ➢ ½ cup flour
- ➢ 1 teaspoon smoky chipotle powder
- ➢ ½ teaspoon ground black pepper
- ➢ 1 teaspoon sea salt flakes
- ➢ 2 eggs, beaten
- ➢ ½ cup crushed saltines
- ➢ 10 ounces (283 g) wax beans
- ➢ Cooking spray

Instructions

1. Preheat the air fryer to 360°F (182°C). 2. Combine the flour, chipotle powder, black pepper, and salt in a bowl. Put the eggs in a second bowl. Put the crushed saltines in a third bowl. 3. Wash the beans with cold water and discard any tough strings. 4. Coat the beans with the flour mixture, before dipping them into the beaten egg. Cover them with the crushed saltines. 5. Spritz the beans with cooking spray. 6. Air fry for 4 minutes. Give the air fryer basket a good shake and continue to air fry for 3 minutes. Serve hot.

Roasted Brussels Sprouts with Bacon

Preparation time: 10 minutes | Cook

time: 20 minutes | Serves 4

- ➤ 4 slices thick-cut bacon, chopped (about ¼ pound / 113 g)
- ➤ 1 pound (454 g) Brussels sprouts, halved (or quartered if large)
- ➤ Freshly ground black pepper, to taste

Instructions

1. Preheat the air fryer to 380°F (193°C). 2. Air fry the bacon for 5 minutes, shaking the basket once or twice during the cooking time. 3. Add the Brussels sprouts to the basket and drizzle a little bacon fat from the bottom of the air fryer drawer into the basket. Toss the sprouts to coat with the bacon fat. Air fry for an additional 15 minutes, or until the Brussels sprouts are tender to a knifepoint. 4. Season with freshly ground black pepper.

Parmesan Mushrooms

Preparation time: 5 minutes | Cook time: 15 minutes | Serves 4

- ➤ Oil, for spraying
- ➤ 1 pound (454 g) cremini mushrooms, stems trimmed
- ➤ 2 tablespoons olive oil
- ➤ 2 teaspoons granulated garlic
- ➤ 1 teaspoon dried onion soup mix
- ➤ ½ teaspoon salt
- ➤ ¼ teaspoon freshly ground black pepper
- ➤ ⅓ cup grated Parmesan cheese, divided

Instructions

1. Line the air fryer basket with parchment and spray lightly with oil. 2. In a large bowl, toss the mushrooms with the olive oil, garlic, onion soup mix, salt, and black pepper until evenly coated. 3. Place the mushrooms in the prepared basket. 4. Roast at 370°F (188°C) for 13 minutes. 5. Sprinkle half of the cheese over the mushrooms and cook for another 2 minutes. 6. Transfer the mushrooms to a serving bowl, add the remaining Parmesan cheese, and toss until evenly coated. Serve immediately.

Golden Garlicky Mushrooms

Preparation time: 10 minutes | Cook time: 10 minutes | Serves 4

- ➤ 6 small mushrooms

- ➤ 1 tablespoon bread crumbs
- ➤ 1 tablespoon olive oil
- ➤ 1 ounce (28 g) onion, peeled and diced
- ➤ 1 teaspoon parsley
- ➤ 1 teaspoon garlic purée
- ➤ Salt and ground black pepper, to taste

Instructions

1. Preheat the air fryer to 350°F (177°C). 2. Combine the bread crumbs, oil, onion, parsley, salt, pepper and garlic in a bowl. Cut out the mushrooms' stalks and stuff each cap with the crumb mixture. 3. Air fry in the air fryer for 10 minutes. 4. Serve hot.

Garlic Parmesan-Roasted Cauliflower

Preparation time: 5 minutes | Cook time: 15 minutes | Serves 6

- ➤ 1 medium head cauliflower, leaves and core removed, cut into florets
- ➤ 2 tablespoons salted butter, melted
- ➤ ½ tablespoon salt
- ➤ 2 cloves garlic, peeled and finely minced
- ➤ ½ cup grated Parmesan cheese, divided

Instructions

1. Toss cauliflower in a large bowl with butter. Sprinkle with salt, garlic, and ¼ cup Parmesan. 2. Place florets into ungreased air fryer basket. Adjust the temperature to 350°F (177°C) and roast for 15 minutes, shaking basket halfway through cooking. Cauliflower will be browned at the edges and tender when done. 3. Transfer florets to a large serving dish and sprinkle with remaining Parmesan. Serve warm.

Ricotta Potatoes

Preparation time: 15 minutes | Cook time: 15 minutes | Serves 4

- ➤ 4 potatoes
- ➤ 2 tablespoons olive oil
- ➤ ½ cup Ricotta cheese, at room temperature
- ➤ 2 tablespoons chopped scallions
- ➤ 1 tablespoon roughly chopped fresh parsley
- ➤ 1 tablespoon minced coriander

- ➤ 2 ounces (57 g) Cheddar cheese, preferably freshly grated
- ➤ 1 teaspoon celery seeds
- ➤ ½ teaspoon salt
- ➤ ½ teaspoon garlic pepper

Instructions

1. Preheat the air fryer to 350°F (177°C). 2. Pierce the skin of the potatoes with a knife. 3. Air fry in the air fryer basket for 13 minutes. If they are not cooked through by this time, leave for 2 to 3 minutes longer. 4. In the meantime, make the stuffing by combining all the other ingredients. 5. Cut halfway into the cooked potatoes to open them. 6. Spoon equal amounts of the stuffing into each potato and serve hot.

Bacon Potatoes and Green Beans

Preparation time: 10 minutes | Cook time: 25 minutes | Serves 4

- ➤ Oil, for spraying
- ➤ 2 pounds (907 g) medium russet potatoes, quartered
- ➤ ¾ cup bacon bits
- ➤ 10 ounces (283 g) fresh green beans
- ➤ 1 teaspoon salt
- ➤ ½ teaspoon freshly ground black pepper

Instructions

1. Line the air fryer basket with parchment and spray lightly with oil. 2. Place the potatoes in the prepared basket. Top with the bacon bits and green beans. Sprinkle with the salt and black pepper and spray liberally with oil. 3. Air fry at 355°F (179°C) for 25 minutes, stirring after 12 minutes and spraying with oil, until the potatoes are easily pierced with a fork.

Broccoli with Sesame Dressing

Preparation time: 5 minutes | Cook time: 10 minutes | Serves 4

- ➤ 6 cups broccoli florets, cut into bite-size pieces
- ➤ 1 tablespoon olive oil
- ➤ ¼ teaspoon salt
- ➤ 2 tablespoons sesame seeds
- ➤ 2 tablespoons rice vinegar
- ➤ 2 tablespoons coconut aminos

- ➤ 2 tablespoons sesame oil
- ➤ ½ teaspoon Swerve
- ➤ ¼ teaspoon red pepper flakes (optional)

Instructions

1. Preheat the air fryer to 400°F (204°C). 2. In a large bowl, toss the broccoli with the olive oil and salt until thoroughly coated. 3. Transfer the broccoli to the air fryer basket. Pausing halfway through the cooking time to shake the basket, air fry for 10 minutes until the stems are tender and the edges are beginning to crisp. 4. Meanwhile, in the same large bowl, whisk together the sesame seeds, vinegar, coconut aminos, sesame oil, Swerve, and red pepper flakes (if using). 5. Transfer the broccoli to the bowl and toss until thoroughly coated with the seasonings. Serve warm or at room temperature.

Broccoli Tots

Preparation time: 15 minutes | Cook time: 10 minutes | Makes 24 tots

- ➤ 2 cups broccoli florets (about ½ pound / 227 g broccoli crowns)
- ➤ 1 egg, beaten
- ➤ ⅛ teaspoon onion powder
- ➤ ¼ teaspoon salt
- ➤ ⅛ teaspoon pepper
- ➤ 2 tablespoons grated Parmesan cheese
- ➤ ¼ cup panko bread crumbs
- ➤ Oil for misting

Instructions

1. Steam broccoli for 2 minutes. Rinse in cold water, drain well, and chop finely. 2. In a large bowl, mix broccoli with all other ingredients except the oil. 3. Scoop out small portions of mixture and shape into 24 tots. Lay them on a cookie sheet or wax paper as you work. 4. Spray tots with oil and place in air fryer basket in single layer. 5. Air fry at 390°F (199°C) for 5 minutes. Shake basket and spray with oil again. Cook 5 minutes longer or until browned and crispy.

Garlic Zucchini and Red Peppers

Preparation time: 5 minutes | Cook time: 15 minutes | Serves 6

- ➤ 2 medium zucchini, cubed
- ➤ 1 red bell pepper, diced

- ➢ 2 garlic cloves, sliced
- ➢ 2 tablespoons olive oil
- ➢ ½ teaspoon salt

Instructions

1. Preheat the air fryer to 380°F(193°C). 2. In a large bowl, mix together the zucchini, bell pepper, and garlic with the olive oil and salt. 3. Pour the mixture into the air fryer basket, and roast for 7 minutes. Shake or stir, then roast for 7 to 8 minutes more.

Cauliflower with Lime Juice

Preparation time: 10 minutes | Cook time: 7 minutes | Serves 4

- ➢ 2 cups chopped cauliflower florets
- ➢ 2 tablespoons coconut oil, melted
- ➢ 2 teaspoons chili powder
- ➢ ½ teaspoon garlic powder
- ➢ 1 medium lime
- ➢ 2 tablespoons chopped cilantro

Instructions

1. In a large bowl, toss cauliflower with coconut oil. Sprinkle with chili powder and garlic powder. Place seasoned cauliflower into the air fryer basket. 2. Adjust the temperature to 350°F (177°C) and set the timer for 7 minutes. 3. Cauliflower will be tender and begin to turn golden at the edges. Place into a serving bowl. 4. Cut the lime into quarters and squeeze juice over cauliflower. Garnish with cilantro.

Broccoli Salad

Preparation time: 5 minutes | Cook time: 7 minutes | Serves 4

- ➢ 2 cups fresh broccoli florets, chopped
- ➢ 1 tablespoon olive oil
- ➢ ¼ teaspoon salt
- ➢ ⅛ teaspoon ground black pepper
- ➢ ¼ cup lemon juice, divided
- ➢ ¼ cup shredded Parmesan cheese
- ➢ ¼ cup sliced roasted almonds

Instructions

1. In a large bowl, toss broccoli and olive oil together. Sprinkle with salt and pepper, then drizzle with 2 tablespoons lemon juice. 2. Place broccoli into ungreased air fryer basket. Adjust the temperature to 350°F (177°C) and set the timer for 7 minutes, shaking the basket halfway through cooking. Broccoli will be golden on the edges when done. 3. Place broccoli into a large serving bowl and drizzle with remaining lemon juice. Sprinkle with Parmesan and almonds. Serve warm.

Bacon-Wrapped Asparagus

Preparation time: 10 minutes | Cook time: 10 minutes | Serves 4

- ➢ 8 slices reduced-sodium bacon, cut in half
- ➢ 16 thick (about 1 pound / 454 g) asparagus spears, trimmed of woody ends

Instructions

1. Preheat the air fryer to 350°F (177°C). 2. Wrap a half piece of bacon around the center of each stalk of asparagus. 3. Working in batches, if necessary, arrange seam-side down in a single layer in the air fryer basket. Air fry for 10 minutes until the bacon is crisp and the stalks are tender.

Buttery Mushrooms

Preparation time: 10 minutes | Cook time: 10 minutes | Serves 4

- ➢ 8 ounces (227 g) cremini mushrooms, halved
- ➢ 2 tablespoons salted butter, melted
- ➢ ¼ teaspoon salt
- ➢ ¼ teaspoon ground black pepper

Instructions

1. In a medium bowl, toss mushrooms with butter, then sprinkle with salt and pepper. Place into ungreased air fryer basket. Adjust the temperature to 400°F (204°C) and air fry for 10 minutes, shaking the basket halfway through cooking. Mushrooms will be tender when done. Serve warm.

Burger Bun for One

Preparation time: 2 minutes | Cook time: 5 minutes | Serves 1

- ➢ 2 tablespoons salted butter, melted
- ➢ ¼ cup blanched finely ground almond flour
- ➢ ¼ teaspoon baking powder

- ➤ ⅛ teaspoon apple cider vinegar
- ➤ 1 large egg, whisked

Instructions

1. Pour butter into an ungreased ramekin. Add flour, baking powder, and vinegar to ramekin and stir until combined. Add egg and stir until batter is mostly smooth. 2. Place ramekin into air fryer basket. Adjust the temperature to 350°F (177°C) and bake for 5 minutes. When done, the center will be firm and the top slightly browned. Let cool, about 5 minutes, then remove from ramekin and slice in half. Serve.

Butternut Squash Croquettes

Preparation time: 5 minutes | Cook time: 17 minutes | Serves 4

- ➤ ⅓ butternut squash, peeled and grated
- ➤ ⅓ cup all-purpose flour
- ➤ 2 eggs, whisked
- ➤ 4 cloves garlic, minced
- ➤ 1½ tablespoons olive oil
- ➤ 1 teaspoon fine sea salt
- ➤ ⅓ teaspoon freshly ground black pepper, or more to taste
- ➤ ⅓ teaspoon dried sage
- ➤ A pinch of ground allspice

Instructions

1. Preheat the air fryer to 345°F (174°C). Line the air fryer basket with parchment paper. 2. In a mixing bowl, stir together all the ingredients until well combined. 3. Make the squash croquettes: Use a small cookie scoop to drop tablespoonfuls of the squash mixture onto a lightly floured surface and shape into balls with your hands. Transfer them to the air fryer basket. 4. Air fry for 17 minutes until the squash croquettes are golden brown. 5. Remove from the basket to a plate and serve warm.

Roasted Sweet Potatoes

Preparation time: 10 minutes | Cook time: 25 minutes | Serves 4

- ➤ Cooking oil spray
- ➤ 2 sweet potatoes, peeled and cut into 1-inch cubes
- ➤ 1 tablespoon extra-virgin olive oil
- ➤ Pinch salt
- ➤ Freshly ground black pepper, to taste
- ➤ ½ teaspoon dried thyme
- ➤ ½ teaspoon dried marjoram
- ➤ ¼ cup grated Parmesan cheese

Instructions

1. Insert the crisper plate into the basket and the basket into the unit. Preheat the unit by selecting AIR ROAST, setting the temperature to 330°F (166°C), and setting the time to 3 minutes. Select START/STOP to begin. 2. Once the unit is preheated, spray the crisper plate with cooking oil. Put the sweet potato cubes into the basket and drizzle with olive oil. Toss gently to coat. Sprinkle with the salt, pepper, thyme, and marjoram and toss again. 3. Select AIR ROAST, set the temperature to 330°F (166°C), and set the time to 25 minutes. Select START/STOP to begin. 4. After 10 minutes, remove the basket and shake the potatoes. Reinsert the basket to resume cooking. After another 10 minutes, remove the basket and shake the potatoes one more time. Sprinkle evenly with the Parmesan cheese. Reinsert the basket to resume cooking. 5. When the cooking is complete, the potatoes should be tender. Serve immediately.

● CHAPTER 9 Vegetarian Mains

Teriyaki Cauliflower

Preparation time: 5 minutes | Cook time: 14 minutes | Serves 4

- ➢ ½ cup soy sauce
- ➢ ⅓ cup water
- ➢ 1 tablespoon brown sugar
- ➢ 1 teaspoon sesame oil
- ➢ 1 teaspoon cornstarch
- ➢ 2 cloves garlic, chopped
- ➢ ½ teaspoon chili powder
- ➢ 1 big cauliflower head, cut into florets

Instructions

1. Preheat the air fryer to 340°F (171°C). 2. Make the teriyaki sauce: In a small bowl, whisk together the soy sauce, water, brown sugar, sesame oil, cornstarch, garlic, and chili powder until well combined. 3. Place the cauliflower florets in a large bowl and drizzle the top with the prepared teriyaki sauce and toss to coat well. 4. Put the cauliflower florets in the air fryer basket and air fry for 14 minutes, shaking the basket halfway through, or until the cauliflower is crisp-tender. 5. Let the cauliflower cool for 5 minutes before serving.

Crispy Tofu

Preparation time: 30 minutes | Cook time: 15 to 20 minutes | Serves 4

- ➢ 1 (16-ounce / 454-g) block extra-firm tofu
- ➢ 2 tablespoons coconut aminos
- ➢ 1 tablespoon toasted sesame oil
- ➢ 1 tablespoon olive oil
- ➢ 1 tablespoon chili-garlic sauce
- ➢ 1½ teaspoons black sesame seeds
- ➢ 1 scallion, thinly sliced

Instructions

1. Press the tofu for at least 15 minutes by wrapping it in paper towels and setting a heavy pan on top so that the moisture drains. 2. Slice the tofu into bite-size cubes and transfer to a bowl. Drizzle with the coconut aminos, sesame oil, olive oil, and chili-garlic sauce. Cover and refrigerate for 1 hour or up to overnight. 3. Preheat the air fryer to 400°F (204°C). 4. Arrange the tofu in a single layer in the air fryer basket. Pausing to shake the pan halfway through the cooking time, air fry for 15 to 20 minutes until crisp. Serve with any juices that accumulate in the bottom of the air fryer, sprinkled with the sesame seeds and sliced scallion.

Tangy Asparagus and Broccoli

Preparation time: 25 minutes | Cook time: 22 minutes | Serves 4

- ➢ ½ pound (227 g) asparagus, cut into 1½-inch pieces
- ➢ ½ pound (227 g) broccoli, cut into 1½-inch pieces
- ➢ 2 tablespoons olive oil
- ➢ Salt and white pepper, to taste
- ➢ ½ cup vegetable broth
- ➢ 2 tablespoons apple cider vinegar

Instructions

1. Place the vegetables in a single layer in the lightly greased air fryer basket. Drizzle the olive oil over the vegetables. 2. Sprinkle with salt and white pepper. 3. Cook at 380°F (193°C) for 15 minutes, shaking the basket halfway through the cooking time. 4. Add ½ cup of vegetable broth to a saucepan; bring to a rapid boil and add the vinegar. Cook for 5 to 7 minutes or until the sauce has reduced by half. 5. Spoon the sauce over the warm vegetables and serve immediately. Bon appétit!

Cauliflower, Chickpea, and Avocado Mash

Preparation time: 10 minutes | Cook time: 25 minutes | Serves 4

- ➢ 1 medium head cauliflower, cut into florets

- 1 can chickpeas, drained and rinsed
- 1 tablespoon extra-virgin olive oil
- 2 tablespoons lemon juice
- Salt and ground black pepper, to taste
- 4 flatbreads, toasted
- 2 ripe avocados, mashed

Instructions

1. Preheat the air fryer to 425°F (218°C). 2. In a bowl, mix the chickpeas, cauliflower, lemon juice and olive oil. Sprinkle salt and pepper as desired. 3. Put inside the air fryer basket and air fry for 25 minutes. 4. Spread on top of the flatbread along with the mashed avocado. Sprinkle with more pepper and salt and serve.

Baked Zucchini

Preparation time: 10 minutes | Cook time: 8 minutes | Serves 4

- 2 tablespoons salted butter
- ¼ cup diced white onion
- ½ teaspoon minced garlic
- ½ cup heavy whipping cream
- 2 ounces (57 g) full-fat cream cheese
- 1 cup shredded sharp Cheddar cheese
- 2 medium zucchini, spiralized

Instructions

1. In a large saucepan over medium heat, melt butter. Add onion and sauté until it begins to soften, 1 to 3 minutes. Add garlic and sauté for 30 seconds, then pour in cream and add cream cheese. 2. Remove the pan from heat and stir in Cheddar. Add the zucchini and toss in the sauce, then put into a round baking dish. Cover the dish with foil and place into the air fryer basket. 3. Adjust the temperature to 370°F (188°C) and set the timer for 8 minutes. 4. After 6 minutes remove the foil and let the top brown for remaining cooking time. Stir and serve.

Whole Roasted Lemon Cauliflower

Preparation time: 5 minutes | Cook time: 15 minutes | Serves 4

- 1 medium head cauliflower
- 2 tablespoons salted butter, melted

- 1 medium lemon
- ½ teaspoon garlic powder
- 1 teaspoon dried parsley

Instructions

1. Remove the leaves from the head of cauliflower and brush it with melted butter. Cut the lemon in half and zest one half onto the cauliflower. Squeeze the juice of the zested lemon half and pour it over the cauliflower. 2. Sprinkle with garlic powder and parsley. Place cauliflower head into the air fryer basket. 3. Adjust the temperature to 350°F (177°C) and air fry for 15 minutes. 4. Check cauliflower every 5 minutes to avoid overcooking. It should be fork tender. 5. To serve, squeeze juice from other lemon half over cauliflower. Serve immediately.

Stuffed Portobellos

Preparation time: 10 minutes | Cook time: 8 minutes | Serves 4

- 3 ounces (85 g) cream cheese, softened
- ½ medium zucchini, trimmed and chopped
- ¼ cup seeded and chopped red bell pepper
- 1½ cups chopped fresh spinach leaves
- 4 large portobello mushrooms, stems removed
- 2 tablespoons coconut oil, melted
- ½ teaspoon salt

Instructions

1. In a medium bowl, mix cream cheese, zucchini, pepper, and spinach. 2. Drizzle mushrooms with coconut oil and sprinkle with salt. Scoop ¼ zucchini mixture into each mushroom. 3. Place mushrooms into ungreased air fryer basket. Adjust the temperature to 400°F (204°C) and air fry for 8 minutes. Portobellos will be tender and tops will be browned when done. Serve warm.

Crispy Eggplant Slices with Parsley

Preparation time: 5 minutes | Cook time: 10 to 12 minutes | Serves 4

- 1 cup flour

- 4 eggs
- Salt, to taste
- 2 cups bread crumbs
- 1 teaspoon Italian seasoning
- 2 eggplants, sliced
- 2 garlic cloves, sliced
- 2 tablespoons chopped parsley
- Cooking spray

Instructions

1. Preheat the air fryer to 390°F (199°C). Spritz the air fryer basket with cooking spray. 2. On a plate, place the flour. In a shallow bowl, whisk the eggs with salt. In another shallow bowl, combine the bread crumbs and Italian seasoning. 3. Dredge the eggplant slices, one at a time, in the flour, then in the whisked eggs, finally in the bread crumb mixture to coat well. 4. Arrange the coated eggplant slices in the air fryer basket and air fry for 10 to 12 minutes until golden brown and crispy. Flip the eggplant slices halfway through the cooking time. 5. Transfer the eggplant slices to a plate and sprinkle the garlic and parsley on top before serving.

Cheese Stuffed Peppers

Preparation time: 20 minutes | Cook time: 15 minutes | Serves 2

- 1 red bell pepper, top and seeds removed
- 1 yellow bell pepper, top and seeds removed
- Salt and pepper, to taste
- 1 cup Cottage cheese
- 4 tablespoons mayonnaise
- 2 pickles, chopped

Instructions

1. Arrange the peppers in the lightly greased air fryer basket. Cook in the preheated air fryer at 400°F (204°C) for 15 minutes, turning them over halfway through the cooking time. 2. Season with salt and pepper. Then, in a mixing bowl, combine the cream cheese with the mayonnaise and chopped pickles. Stuff the pepper with the cream cheese mixture and serve. Enjoy!

Broccoli with Garlic Sauce

Preparation time: 19 minutes | Cook

time: 15 minutes | Serves 4

- 2 tablespoons olive oil
- Kosher salt and freshly ground black pepper, to taste
- 1 pound (454 g) broccoli florets
- Dipping Sauce:
- 2 teaspoons dried rosemary, crushed
- 3 garlic cloves, minced
- ⅓ teaspoon dried marjoram, crushed
- ¼ cup sour cream
- ⅓ cup mayonnaise

Instructions

1. Lightly grease your broccoli with a thin layer of olive oil. Season with salt and ground black pepper. 2. Arrange the seasoned broccoli in the air fryer basket. Bake at 395°F (202°C) for 15 minutes, shaking once or twice. In the meantime, prepare the dipping sauce by mixing all the sauce ingredients. Serve warm broccoli with the dipping sauce and enjoy!

Mediterranean Pan Pizza

Preparation time: 5 minutes | Cook time: 8 minutes | Serves 2

- 1 cup shredded Mozzarella cheese
- ¼ medium red bell pepper, seeded and chopped
- ½ cup chopped fresh spinach leaves
- 2 tablespoons chopped black olives
- 2 tablespoons crumbled feta cheese

Instructions

1. Sprinkle Mozzarella into an ungreased round nonstick baking dish in an even layer. Add remaining ingredients on top. 2. Place dish into air fryer basket. Adjust the temperature to 350°F (177°C) and bake for 8 minutes, checking halfway through to avoid burning. Top of pizza will be golden brown and the cheese melted when done. 3. Remove dish from fryer and let cool 5 minutes before slicing and serving.

Cheese Stuffed Zucchini

Preparation time: 20 minutes | Cook time: 8 minutes | Serves 4

- 1 large zucchini, cut into four pieces
- 2 tablespoons olive oil
- 1 cup Ricotta cheese, room temperature

- 2 tablespoons scallions, chopped
- 1 heaping tablespoon fresh parsley, roughly chopped
- 1 heaping tablespoon coriander, minced
- 2 ounces (57 g) Cheddar cheese, preferably freshly grated
- 1 teaspoon celery seeds
- ½ teaspoon salt
- ½ teaspoon garlic pepper

Instructions

1. Cook your zucchini in the air fryer basket for approximately 10 minutes at 350°F (177°C). Check for doneness and cook for 2-3 minutes longer if needed. 2. Meanwhile, make the stuffing by mixing the other items. 3. When your zucchini is thoroughly cooked, open them up. Divide the stuffing among all zucchini pieces and bake an additional 5 minutes.

Super Vegetable Burger

Preparation time: 15 minutes | Cook time: 12 minutes | Serves 8

- ½ pound (227 g) cauliflower, steamed and diced, rinsed and drained
- 2 teaspoons coconut oil, melted
- 2 teaspoons minced garlic
- ¼ cup desiccated coconut
- ½ cup oats
- 3 tablespoons flour
- 1 tablespoon flaxseeds plus 3 tablespoons water, divided
- 1 teaspoon mustard powder
- 2 teaspoons thyme
- 2 teaspoons parsley
- 2 teaspoons chives
- Salt and ground black pepper, to taste
- 1 cup bread crumbs

Instructions

1. Preheat the air fryer to 390°F (199°C). 2. Combine the cauliflower with all the ingredients, except for the bread crumbs, incorporating everything well. 3. Using the hands, shape 8 equal-sized amounts of the mixture into burger patties. Coat the patties in bread crumbs before putting them in the air fryer basket in a single layer. 4. Air fry for 12 minutes or until crispy.

5. Serve hot.

Sweet Pepper Nachos

Preparation time: 10 minutes | Cook time: 5 minutes | Serves 2

- 6 mini sweet peppers, seeded and sliced in half
- ¾ cup shredded Colby jack cheese
- ¼ cup sliced pickled jalapeños
- ½ medium avocado, peeled, pitted, and diced
- 2 tablespoons sour cream

Instructions

1. Place peppers into an ungreased round nonstick baking dish. Sprinkle with Colby and top with jalapeños. 2. Place dish into air fryer basket. Adjust the temperature to 350°F (177°C) and bake for 5 minutes. Cheese will be melted and bubbly when done. 3. Remove dish from air fryer and top with avocado. Drizzle with sour cream. Serve warm.

Fried Root Vegetable Medley with Thyme

Preparation time: 10 minutes | Cook time: 22 minutes | Serves 4

- 2 carrots, sliced
- 2 potatoes, cut into chunks
- 1 rutabaga, cut into chunks
- 1 turnip, cut into chunks
- 1 beet, cut into chunks
- 8 shallots, halved
- 2 tablespoons olive oil
- Salt and black pepper, to taste
- 2 tablespoons tomato pesto
- 2 tablespoons water
- 2 tablespoons chopped fresh thyme

Instructions

1. Preheat the air fryer to 400°F (204°C). 2. Toss the carrots, potatoes, rutabaga, turnip, beet, shallots, olive oil, salt, and pepper in a large mixing bowl until the root vegetables are evenly coated. 3. Place the root vegetables in the air fryer basket and air fry for 12 minutes. Shake the basket and air fry for another 10 minutes until they are cooked to your preferred

doneness. 4. Meanwhile, in a small bowl, whisk together the tomato pesto and water until smooth. 5. When ready, remove the root vegetables from the basket to a platter. Drizzle with the tomato pesto mixture and sprinkle with the thyme. Serve immediately.

Lush Summer Rolls

Preparation time: 15 minutes | Cook time: 15 minutes | Serves 4

- ➤ 1 cup shiitake mushroom, sliced thinly
- ➤ 1 celery stalk, chopped
- ➤ 1 medium carrot, shredded
- ➤ ½ teaspoon finely chopped ginger
- ➤ 1 teaspoon sugar
- ➤ 1 tablespoon soy sauce
- ➤ 1 teaspoon nutritional yeast
- ➤ 8 spring roll sheets
- ➤ 1 teaspoon corn starch
- ➤ 2 tablespoons water

Instructions

1. In a bowl, combine the ginger, soy sauce, nutritional yeast, carrots, celery, mushroom, and sugar. 2. Mix the cornstarch and water to create an adhesive for the spring rolls. 3. Scoop a tablespoonful of the vegetable mixture into the middle of the spring roll sheets. Brush the edges of the sheets with the cornstarch adhesive and enclose around the filling to make spring rolls. 4. Preheat the air fryer to 400°F (204°C). When warm, place the rolls inside and air fry for 15 minutes or until crisp. 5. Serve hot.

Cheesy Cabbage Wedges

Preparation time: 5 minutes | Cook time: 20 minutes | Serves 4

- ➤ 4 tablespoons melted butter
- ➤ 1 head cabbage, cut into wedges
- ➤ 1 cup shredded Parmesan cheese
- ➤ Salt and black pepper, to taste
- ➤ ½ cup shredded Mozzarella cheese

Instructions

1. Preheat the air fryer to 380°F (193°C). 2. Brush the melted butter over the cut sides of cabbage wedges and sprinkle both sides with the Parmesan

cheese. Season with salt and pepper to taste. 3. Place the cabbage wedges in the air fryer basket and air fry for 20 minutes, flipping the cabbage halfway through, or until the cabbage wedges are lightly browned. 4. Transfer the cabbage wedges to a plate and serve with the Mozzarella cheese sprinkled on top.

Roasted Veggie Bowl

Preparation time: 10 minutes | Cook time: 15 minutes | Serves 2

- ➤ 1 cup broccoli florets
- ➤ 1 cup quartered Brussels sprouts
- ➤ ½ cup cauliflower florets
- ➤ ¼ medium white onion, peeled and sliced ¼ inch thick
- ➤ ½ medium green bell pepper, seeded and sliced ¼ inch thick
- ➤ 1 tablespoon coconut oil
- ➤ 2 teaspoons chili powder
- ➤ ½ teaspoon garlic powder
- ➤ ½ teaspoon cumin

Instructions

1. Toss all ingredients together in a large bowl until vegetables are fully coated with oil and seasoning. 2. Pour vegetables into the air fryer basket. 3. Adjust the temperature to 360°F (182°C) and roast for 15 minutes. 4. Shake two or three times during cooking. Serve warm.

Three-Cheese Zucchini Boats

Preparation time: 15 minutes | Cook time: 20 minutes | Serves 2

- ➤ 2 medium zucchini
- ➤ 1 tablespoon avocado oil
- ➤ ¼ cup low-carb, no-sugar-added pasta sauce
- ➤ ¼ cup full-fat ricotta cheese
- ➤ ¼ cup shredded Mozzarella cheese
- ➤ ¼ teaspoon dried oregano
- ➤ ¼ teaspoon garlic powder
- ➤ ½ teaspoon dried parsley
- ➤ 2 tablespoons grated vegetarian Parmesan cheese

Instructions

1. Cut off 1 inch from the top and bottom of each

zucchini. Slice zucchini in half lengthwise and use a spoon to scoop out a bit of the inside, making room for filling. Brush with oil and spoon 2 tablespoons pasta sauce into each shell. 2. In a medium bowl, mix ricotta, Mozzarella, oregano, garlic powder, and parsley. Spoon the mixture into each zucchini shell. Place stuffed zucchini shells into the air fryer basket. 3. Adjust the temperature to 350°F (177°C) and air fry for 20 minutes. 4. To remove from the basket, use tongs or a spatula and carefully lift out. Top with Parmesan. Serve immediately.

Garlic White Zucchini Rolls

Preparation time: 20 minutes | Cook time: 20 minutes | Serves 4

- ➢ 2 medium zucchini
- ➢ 2 tablespoons unsalted butter
- ➢ ¼ white onion, peeled and diced
- ➢ ½ teaspoon finely minced roasted garlic
- ➢ ¼ cup heavy cream
- ➢ 2 tablespoons vegetable broth
- ➢ ⅛ teaspoon xanthan gum
- ➢ ½ cup full-fat ricotta cheese
- ➢ ¼ teaspoon salt
- ➢ ½ teaspoon garlic powder
- ➢ ¼ teaspoon dried oregano
- ➢ 2 cups spinach, chopped
- ➢ ½ cup sliced baby portobello mushrooms
- ➢ ¾ cup shredded Mozzarella cheese, divided

Instructions

1. Using a mandoline or sharp knife, slice zucchini into long strips lengthwise. Place strips between paper towels to absorb moisture. Set aside. 2. In a medium saucepan over medium heat, melt butter. Add onion and sauté until fragrant. Add garlic and sauté 30 seconds. 3. Pour in heavy cream, broth, and xanthan gum. Turn off heat and whisk mixture until it begins to thicken, about 3 minutes. 4. In a medium bowl, add ricotta, salt, garlic powder, and oregano and mix well. Fold in spinach, mushrooms, and ½ cup Mozzarella. 5. Pour half of the sauce into a round baking pan. To assemble the rolls, place two strips of zucchini on a work surface. Spoon 2 tablespoons of ricotta mixture onto the slices and roll up. Place seam side down on top of sauce. Repeat with remaining ingredients. 6. Pour remaining sauce over the rolls and sprinkle with remaining Mozzarella. Cover with foil and place into the air fryer basket. 7. Adjust the temperature to 350°F (177°C) and bake for 20 minutes. 8. In the last 5 minutes, remove the foil to brown the cheese. Serve immediately.

● CHAPTER 10 Treats and Desserts

Maple-Pecan Tart with Sea Salt

Preparation time: 15 minutes | Cook time: 25 minutes | Serves 8

➤ Tart Crust:
➤ Vegetable oil spray
➤ ⅓ cup (⅔ stick) butter, softened
➤ ¼ cup firmly packed brown sugar
➤ 1 cup all-purpose flour
➤ ¼ teaspoon kosher salt
➤ Filling:
➤ 4 tablespoons (½ stick) butter, diced
➤ ½ cup packed brown sugar
➤ ¼ cup pure maple syrup
➤ ¼ cup whole milk
➤ ¼ teaspoon pure vanilla extract
➤ 1½ cups finely chopped pecans
➤ ¼ teaspoon flaked sea salt

Instructions

1. For the crust: Line a baking pan with foil, leaving a couple of inches of overhang. Spray the foil with vegetable oil spray. 2. In a medium bowl, combine the butter and brown sugar. Beat with an electric mixer on medium-low speed until light and fluffy. Add the flour and kosher salt and beat until the ingredients are well blended. Transfer the mixture (it will be crumbly) to the prepared pan. Press it evenly into the bottom of the pan. 3. Place the pan in the air fryer basket. Set the air fryer to 350°F (177°C) for 13 minutes. When the crust has 5 minutes left to cook, start the filling. 4. For the filling: In a medium saucepan, combine the butter, brown sugar, maple syrup, and milk. Bring to a simmer, stirring occasionally. When it begins simmering, cook for 1 minute. Remove from the heat and stir in the vanilla and pecans. 5. Carefully pour the filling evenly over the crust, gently spreading with a rubber spatula so the nuts and liquid are evenly distributed. Set the air fryer to 350°F (177°C) for 12 minutes, or until mixture is bubbling. (The center should still be slightly jiggly, it will thicken as it cools.) 6. Remove the pan from the air fryer and sprinkle the tart with the sea salt. Cool completely on a wire rack until room temperature. 7. Transfer the pan to the refrigerator to chill. When cold (the tart will be easier to cut), use the foil overhang to remove the tart from the pan and cut into 8 wedges. Serve at room temperature.

Cardamom Custard

Preparation time: 10 minutes | Cook time: 25 minutes | Serves 2

➤ 1 cup whole milk
➤ 1 large egg
➤ 2 tablespoons plus 1 teaspoon sugar
➤ ¼ teaspoon vanilla bean paste or pure vanilla extract
➤ ¼ teaspoon ground cardamom, plus more for sprinkling

Instructions

1. In a medium bowl, beat together the milk, egg, sugar, vanilla, and cardamom. 2. Place two 8 ounces (227 g) ramekins in the air fryer basket. Divide the mixture between the ramekins. Sprinkle lightly with cardamom. Cover each ramekin tightly with aluminum foil. Set the air fryer to 350°F (177°C) for 25 minutes, or until a toothpick inserted in the center comes out clean. 3. Let the custards cool on a wire rack for 5 to 10 minutes. 4. Serve warm, or refrigerate until cold and serve chilled.

Bourbon Bread Pudding

Preparation time: 10 minutes | Cook time: 20 minutes | Serves 4

➤ 3 slices whole grain bread, cubed
➤ 1 large egg
➤ 1 cup whole milk
➤ 2 tablespoons bourbon
➤ ½ teaspoons vanilla extract
➤ ¼ cup maple syrup, divided

- ➤ ½ teaspoons ground cinnamon
- ➤ 2 teaspoons sparkling sugar

Instructions

1. Preheat the air fryer to 270°F (132°C). 2. Spray a baking pan with nonstick cooking spray, then place the bread cubes in the pan. 3. In a medium bowl, whisk together the egg, milk, bourbon, vanilla extract, 3 tablespoons of maple syrup, and cinnamon. Pour the egg mixture over the bread and press down with a spatula to coat all the bread, then sprinkle the sparkling sugar on top and bake for 20 minutes. 4. Remove the pudding from the air fryer and allow to cool in the pan on a wire rack for 10 minutes. Drizzle the remaining 1 tablespoon of maple syrup on top. Slice and serve warm.

Chocolate Bread Pudding

Preparation time: 10 minutes | Cook time: 10 to 12 minutes | Serves 4

- ➤ Nonstick flour-infused baking spray
- ➤ 1 egg
- ➤ 1 egg yolk
- ➤ ¾ cup chocolate milk
- ➤ 2 tablespoons cocoa powder
- ➤ 3 tablespoons light brown sugar
- ➤ 3 tablespoons peanut butter
- ➤ 1 teaspoon vanilla extract
- ➤ 5 slices firm white bread, cubed

Instructions

1. Spray a 6-by-2-inch round baking pan with the baking spray. Set aside. 2. In a medium bowl, whisk the egg, egg yolk, chocolate milk, cocoa powder, brown sugar, peanut butter, and vanilla until thoroughly combined. Stir in the bread cubes and let soak for 10 minutes. Spoon this mixture into the prepared pan. 3. Insert the crisper plate into the basket and the basket into the unit. Preheat the unit by selecting BAKE, setting the temperature to 325°F (163°C), and setting the time to 3 minutes. Select START/STOP to begin. 4. Once the unit is preheated, place the pan into the basket. Select BAKE, set the temperature to 325°F (163°C), and set the time to 12 minutes. Select START/STOP to begin. 5. Check the pudding after about 10 minutes. It is done when it is

firm to the touch. If not, resume cooking. 6. When the cooking is complete, let the pudding cool for 5 minutes. Serve warm.

Blackberry Cobbler

Preparation time: 15 minutes | Cook time: 25 to 30 minutes | Serves 6

- ➤ 3 cups fresh or frozen blackberries
- ➤ 1¾ cups sugar, divided
- ➤ 1 teaspoon vanilla extract
- ➤ 8 tablespoons (1 stick) butter, melted
- ➤ 1 cup self-rising flour
- ➤ 1 to 2 tablespoons oil

Instructions

1. In a medium bowl, stir together the blackberries, 1 cup of sugar, and vanilla. 2. In another medium bowl, stir together the melted butter, remaining ¾ cup of sugar, and flour until a dough forms. 3. Spritz a baking pan with oil. Add the blackberry mixture. Crumble the flour mixture over the fruit. Cover the pan with aluminum foil. 4. Preheat the air fryer to 350°F (177°C). 5. Place the covered pan in the air fryer basket. Cook for 20 to 25 minutes until the filling is thickened. 6. Uncover the pan and cook for 5 minutes more, depending on how juicy and browned you like your cobbler. Let sit for 5 minutes before serving.

Strawberry Scone Shortcake

Preparation time: 10 minutes | Cook time: 20 minutes | Serves 4 to 6

- ➤ 1⅓ cups all-purpose flour
- ➤ 3 tablespoons granulated sugar
- ➤ 1½ teaspoons baking powder
- ➤ 1 teaspoon kosher salt
- ➤ 8 tablespoons (1 stick) unsalted butter, cubed and chilled
- ➤ 1⅓ cups heavy cream, chilled
- ➤ Turbinado sugar, for sprinkling
- ➤ 2 tablespoons powdered sugar, plus more for dusting
- ➤ ½ teaspoon vanilla extract
- ➤ 1 cup quartered fresh strawberries

Instructions

1. In a large bowl, whisk together the flour,

granulated sugar, baking powder, and salt. Add the butter and use your fingers to break apart the butter pieces while working them into the flour mixture, until pea-size pieces form. Pour ⅔ cup of the cream over the flour mixture and, using a rubber spatula, mix the ingredients together until just combined. 2. Transfer the dough to a work surface and form into a 7-inch-wide disk. Brush the top with water, then sprinkle with some turbinado sugar. Using a large metal spatula, transfer the dough to the air fryer and bake at 350°F (177°C) until golden brown and fluffy, about 20 minutes. Let cool in the air fryer basket for 5 minutes, then turn out onto a wire rack, right-side up, to cool completely. 3. Meanwhile, in a bowl, beat the remaining ⅔ cup cream, the powdered sugar, and vanilla until stiff peaks form. Split the scone like a hamburger bun and spread the strawberries over the bottom. Top with the whipped cream and cover with the top of the scone. Dust with powdered sugar and cut into wedges to serve.

Glazed Cherry Turnovers

Preparation time: 10 minutes | Cook time: 14 minutes per batch | Serves 8

- ➢ 2 sheets frozen puff pastry, thawed
- ➢ 1 (21 ounces / 595 g) can premium cherry pie filling
- ➢ 2 teaspoons ground cinnamon
- ➢ 1 egg, beaten
- ➢ 1 cup sliced almonds
- ➢ 1 cup powdered sugar
- ➢ 2 tablespoons milk

Instructions

1. Roll a sheet of puff pastry out into a square that is approximately 10-inches by 10-inches. Cut this large square into quarters. 2. Mix the cherry pie filling and cinnamon together in a bowl. Spoon ¼ cup of the cherry filling into the center of each puff pastry square. Brush the perimeter of the pastry square with the egg wash. Fold one corner of the puff pastry over the cherry pie filling towards the opposite corner, forming a triangle. Seal the two edges of the pastry together with the tip of a fork, making a design with the tines. Brush the top of the turnovers

with the egg wash and sprinkle sliced almonds over each one. Repeat these steps with the second sheet of puff pastry. You should have eight turnovers at the end. 3. Preheat the air fryer to 370°F (188°C). 4. Air fry two turnovers at a time for 14 minutes, carefully turning them over halfway through the cooking time. 5. While the turnovers are cooking, make the glaze by whisking the powdered sugar and milk together in a small bowl until smooth. Let the glaze sit for a minute so the sugar can absorb the milk. If the consistency is still too thick to drizzle, add a little more milk, a drop at a time, and stir until smooth. 6. Let the cooked cherry turnovers sit for at least 10 minutes. Then drizzle the glaze over each turnover in a zigzag motion. Serve warm or at room temperature.

Baked Cheesecake

Preparation time: 30 minutes | Cook time: 35 minutes | Serves 6

- ➢ ½ cup almond flour
- ➢ 1½ tablespoons unsalted butter, melted
- ➢ 2 tablespoons erythritol
- ➢ 1 (8 ounces / 227 g) package cream cheese, softened
- ➢ ¼ cup powdered erythritol
- ➢ ½ teaspoon vanilla paste
- ➢ 1 egg, at room temperature
- ➢ Topping:
- ➢ 1½ cups sour cream
- ➢ 3 tablespoons powdered erythritol
- ➢ 1 teaspoon vanilla extract

Instructions

1. Thoroughly combine the almond flour, butter, and 2 tablespoons of erythritol in a mixing bowl. Press the mixture into the bottom of lightly greased custard cups. 2. Then, mix the cream cheese, ¼ cup of powdered erythritol, vanilla, and egg using an electric mixer on low speed. Pour the batter into the pan, covering the crust. 3. Bake in the preheated air fryer at 330°F (166°C) for 35 minutes until edges are puffed and the surface is firm. 4. Mix the sour cream, 3 tablespoons of powdered erythritol, and vanilla for the topping; spread over the crust and allow it to cool

to room temperature. 5. Transfer to your refrigerator for 6 to 8 hours. Serve well chilled.

Pecan Brownies

Preparation time: 10 minutes | Cook time: 20 minutes | Serves 6

- ½ cup blanched finely ground almond flour
- ½ cup powdered erythritol
- 2 tablespoons unsweetened cocoa powder
- ½ teaspoon baking powder
- ¼ cup unsalted butter, softened
- 1 large egg
- ¼ cup chopped pecans
- ¼ cup low-carb, sugar-free chocolate chips

Instructions

1. In a large bowl, mix almond flour, erythritol, cocoa powder, and baking powder. Stir in butter and egg. 2. Fold in pecans and chocolate chips. Scoop mixture into a round baking pan. Place pan into the air fryer basket. 3. Adjust the temperature to 300°F (149°C) and bake for 20 minutes. 4. When fully cooked a toothpick inserted in center will come out clean. Allow 20 minutes to fully cool and firm up.

Vanilla Scones

Preparation time: 20 minutes | Cook time: 10 minutes | Serves 6

- 4 ounces (113 g) coconut flour
- ½ teaspoon baking powder
- 1 teaspoon apple cider vinegar
- 2 teaspoons mascarpone
- ¼ cup heavy cream
- 1 teaspoon vanilla extract
- 1 tablespoon erythritol
- Cooking spray

Instructions

1. In the mixing bowl, mix coconut flour with baking powder, apple cider vinegar, mascarpone, heavy cream, vanilla extract, and erythritol. 2. Knead the dough and cut into scones. 3. Then put them in the air fryer basket and sprinkle with cooking spray. 4. Cook the vanilla scones at 365°F (185°C) for 10

minutes.

Pecan Clusters

Preparation time: 10 minutes | Cook time: 8 minutes | Serves 8

- 3 ounces (85 g) whole shelled pecans
- 1 tablespoon salted butter, melted
- 2 teaspoons confectioners' erythritol
- ½ teaspoon ground cinnamon
- ½ cup low-carb chocolate chips

Instructions

1. In a medium bowl, toss pecans with butter, then sprinkle with erythritol and cinnamon. 2. Place pecans into ungreased air fryer basket. Adjust the temperature to 350°F (177°C) and air fry for 8 minutes, shaking the basket two times during cooking. They will feel soft initially but get crunchy as they cool. 3. Line a large baking sheet with parchment paper. 4. Place chocolate in a medium microwave-safe bowl. Microwave on high, heating in 20-second increments and stirring until melted. Place 1 teaspoon chocolate in a rounded mound on ungreased parchment-lined baking sheet, then press 1 pecan into top, repeating with remaining chocolate and pecans. 5. Place baking sheet into refrigerator to cool at least 30 minutes. Once cooled, store clusters in a large sealed container in refrigerator up to 5 days.

Dark Brownies

Preparation time: 10 minutes | Cook time: 11 to 13 minutes | Serves 4

- 1 egg
- ½ cup granulated sugar
- ¼ teaspoon salt
- ½ teaspoon vanilla
- ¼ cup butter, melted
- ¼ cup flour, plus 2 tablespoons
- ¼ cup cocoa
- Cooking spray
- Optional:
- Vanilla ice cream
- Caramel sauce
- Whipped cream

Instructions

1. Beat together egg, sugar, salt, and vanilla until light. 2. Add melted butter and mix well. 3. Stir in flour and cocoa. 4. Spray a baking pan lightly with cooking spray. 5. Spread batter in pan and bake at 330°F (166°C) for 11 to 13 minutes. Cool and cut into 4 large squares or 16 small brownie bites.

Peach Cobbler

Preparation time: 15 minutes | Cook time: 12 to 14 minutes | Serves 4

- 16 ounces (454 g) frozen peaches, thawed, with juice (do not drain)
- 6 tablespoons sugar
- 1 tablespoon cornstarch
- 1 tablespoon water
- Crust:
- ½ cup flour
- ¼ teaspoon salt
- 3 tablespoons butter
- 1½ tablespoons cold water
- ¼ teaspoon sugar

Instructions

1. Place peaches, including juice, and sugar in a baking pan. Stir to mix well. 2. In a small cup, dissolve cornstarch in the water. Stir into peaches. 3. In a medium bowl, combine the flour and salt. Cut in butter using knives or a pastry blender. Stir in the cold water to make a stiff dough. 4. On a floured board or wax paper, pat dough into a square or circle slightly smaller than your baking pan. Cut diagonally into 4 pieces. 5. Place dough pieces on top of peaches, leaving a tiny bit of space between the edges. Sprinkle very lightly with sugar, no more than about ¼ teaspoon. 6. Bake at 360°F (182°C) for 12 to 14 minutes, until fruit bubbles and crust browns.

Dark Chocolate Lava Cake

Preparation time: 5 minutes | Cook time: 10 minutes | Serves 4

- Olive oil cooking spray
- ¼ cup whole wheat flour
- 1 tablespoon unsweetened dark chocolate cocoa powder
- ⅛ teaspoon salt
- ½ teaspoon baking powder

- ¼ cup raw honey
- 1 egg
- 2 tablespoons olive oil

Instructions

1. Preheat the air fryer to 380°F(193°C). Lightly coat the insides of four ramekins with olive oil cooking spray. 2. In a medium bowl, combine the flour, cocoa powder, salt, baking powder, honey, egg, and olive oil. 3. Divide the batter evenly among the ramekins. 4. Place the filled ramekins inside the air fryer and bake for 10 minutes. 5. Remove the lava cakes from the air fryer and slide a knife around the outside edge of each cake. Turn each ramekin upside down on a saucer and serve.

Olive Oil Cake

Preparation time: 10 minutes | Cook time: 30 minutes | Serves 8

- 2 cups blanched finely ground almond flour
- 5 large eggs, whisked
- ¾ cup extra-virgin olive oil
- ⅓ cup granular erythritol
- 1 teaspoon vanilla extract
- 1 teaspoon baking powder

Instructions

1. In a large bowl, mix all ingredients. Pour batter into an ungreased round nonstick baking dish. 2. Place dish into air fryer basket. Adjust the temperature to 300°F (149°C) and bake for 30 minutes. The cake will be golden on top and firm in the center when done. 3. Let cake cool in dish 30 minutes before slicing and serving.

Peach Fried Pies

Preparation time: 15 minutes | Cook time: 20 minutes | Makes 8 pies

- 1 (14.75-ounce / 418-g) can sliced peaches in heavy syrup
- 1 teaspoon ground cinnamon
- 1 tablespoon cornstarch
- 1 large egg
- All-purpose flour, for dusting
- 2 refrigerated piecrusts

Instructions

1. Reserving 2 tablespoons of syrup, drain the peaches well. Chop the peaches into bite-size pieces, transfer to a medium bowl, and stir in the cinnamon. 2. In a small bowl, stir together the reserved peach juice and cornstarch until dissolved. Stir this slurry into the peaches. 3. In another small bowl, beat the egg. 4. Dust a cutting board or work surface with flour and spread the piecrusts on the prepared surface. Using a knife, cut each crust into 4 squares (8 squares total). 5. Place 2 tablespoons of peaches onto each dough square. Fold the dough in half and seal the edges. Using a pastry brush, spread the beaten egg on both sides of each hand pie. Using a knife, make 2 thin slits in the top of each pie. 6. Preheat the air fryer to 350°F (177°C). 7. Line the air fryer basket with parchment paper. Place 4 pies on the parchment. 8. Cook for 10 minutes. Flip the pies, brush with beaten egg, and cook for 5 minutes more. Repeat with the remaining pies.

Chocolate Chip Cookie Cake

Preparation time: 5 minutes | Cook time: 15 minutes | Serves 8

- ➤ 4 tablespoons salted butter, melted
- ➤ ⅓ cup granular brown erythritol
- ➤ 1 large egg
- ➤ ½ teaspoon vanilla extract
- ➤ 1 cup blanched finely ground almond flour
- ➤ ½ teaspoon baking powder
- ➤ ¼ cup low-carb chocolate chips

Instructions

1. In a large bowl, whisk together butter, erythritol, egg, and vanilla. Add flour and baking powder, and stir until combined. 2. Fold in chocolate chips, then spoon batter into an ungreased round nonstick baking dish. 3. Place dish into air fryer basket. Adjust the temperature to 300°F (149°C) and set the timer for 15 minutes. When edges are browned, cookie cake will be done. 4. Slice and serve warm.

• Appendix 1: Measurement Conversion Chart

Volume Equivalents (Dry):	Temperature Equivalents:
1/8 teaspoon = 0.5 mL	225°F = 107°C
1/4 teaspoon = 1 mL	250°F = 121°C
1/2 teaspoon = 2 mL	275°F = 135°C
3/4 teaspoon = 4 mL	300°F = 149°C
1 teaspoon = 5 mL	325°F = 163°C
1 tablespoon = 15 mL	350°F = 177°C
1/4 cup = 59 mL	375°F = 191°C
1/2 cup = 118 mL	400°F = 204°C
3/4 cup = 177 mL	425°F = 218°C
1 cup = 235 mL	450°F = 232°C
2 cups (or 1 pint) = 475 mL	475°F = 246°C
4 cups (or 1 quart) = 1 L	500°F = 260°C

Weight Equivalents:	Volume Equivalents (Liquid):
1 ounce = 28 g	1/4 cup = 60 mL = 2 fl oz
2 ounces = 57 g	1/2 cup = 120 mL = 4 fl oz
5 ounces = 142 g	1 cup = 240 mL = 8 fl oz
10 ounces = 284 g	2 cups (or 1 pint) = 475 mL = 16 fl oz
15 ounces = 425 g	4 cups (or 1 quart) = 1 L = 32 fl oz
16 ounces (1 pound) = 455 g	1 gallon = 4 L = 128 fl oz
1.5 pounds = 680 g	
2 pounds = 907 g	

● Appendix 2: Recipe Index

Made in the USA
Coppell, TX
12 December 2024

42075992R00050